BrandVision Marketing Presents…

Local Branding Blueprint--
A Strategic Guide to Increasing
Visibility, Trust & Market Authority

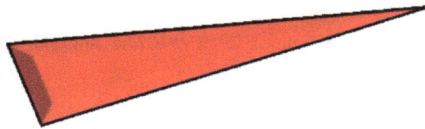

By Scott Trueblood

BVM
Publishing

Library of Congress Control Number: 2025922816

Published by:

BVM Publishing * 8913 Town & Country Circle /#1077 * Knoxville, TN 37923

Author: Matthew Scott Trueblood

Printed and bound in the United States of America.

ISBN 978-0-9840665-2-0

Table of Contents

Local Branding Blueprint: A Strategic Guide to Increasing Visibility, Trust & Market Authority

Preface

Welcome to *Local Branding Blueprint: A Strategic Guide to Increasing Visibility, Trust & Market Authority.* This is your practical playbook for building a powerful, authentic brand that thrives in your local community.

Let's be honest—studying Coca-Cola, Nike, Microsoft, Apple, Starbucks, and McDonald's can teach you plenty about branding principles. But trying to copy them in a local market? That's a one-way ticket to a costly "learning experience" (and an expensive reminder that your budget is a distant guarantee from a Super Bowl ad slot).

Big brands have deep pockets, global reach, and armies of marketers. You have focus, community ties, and the ability to connect directly with your audience in a way they can't…in a very personal, relationship-centric way. That's your edge.

I started BrandVision Marketing in 1993 while selling radio advertising for a local NewsTalk station. I wasn't your typical salesperson—I'd rather talk about the client's *entire* marketing picture than make a pitch. Eventually, that approach became my business model. In 1998, BrandVision Marketing evolved into a full-service agency with one core belief: a strong brand identity is the most valuable asset you can own, especially in a local market.

Why branding? Marketing and advertising often carry a negative reputation—pushy, salesy, deceptive, and impersonal. While marketing and advertising are core components of branding, branding itself is fundamentally different. Branding is the heart of your business made visible. It's about creating relationships, not just transactions. And in a local market, those relationships become your currency. It's the currency of connection…with the consumer, individually, as well as collectively on Main Street, and possibly beyond. Branding forces you to stand for something…and something good…something positive. It speaks to the very heart of what business is supposed to be about: Relationship.

If you read *Digital Marketing Blueprint*, you already know I'm a Salem, Indiana boy…University of Tennessee grad and Vols loyalist. You might remember that my friends call me "True"…that I'm a Star Wars nerd, Yankees fan and lifelong animal lover. What you may not know is that my perspective on branding and relationships comes from more than boardrooms and marketing campaigns—it's rooted in family.

My mom passed away when I was 15, and my dad was tragically killed in a car accident nine years later. Those losses taught me early on that relationships are fragile, but they're also the most important thing we leave behind. That belief shapes how I see branding—not just as logos and slogans, but as lasting connections people can count on.

Simply put, branding is about relationships.

I dedicate this book to my parents because they taught me to value relationships over transactions, to appreciate the moments that matter, and to recognize that people are at the heart of every story—including every brand story.

I've included a couple of family photos here—not to serve as a tearjerker by any stretch, but to give you a glimpse of the real me. The kid at the breakfast counter with his mom and sister…later the 16-year-old goofy teen in Hawaii with his dad, sister, and brother-in-law (Man, I miss that hat!). Those memories remind me daily why relationships matter most—and why local branding is about so much more than marketing.

(LEFT: Me, Mom, and my sister at the breakfast counter — mornings like these taught me more about connection than any textbook ever could…not to mention how to focus on my cereal and not get caught up in the incessant 'picking' that my older sib dished out! RIGHT: With Dad, my sister, and brother-in-law in Hawaii — a reminder that the best memories, like the best brands, are built on relationships that last.)

That's part of why this book is so personal to me. Branding is about connection, about how people remember you and what you stand for. It's about building something lasting that people can count on, even when the rest of life feels unpredictable.

Over the years, I've worked with brands of all shapes and sizes—researching their direction, defining their identity, training their teams, and building brand-centric marketing plans that drive revenue month after month. That's the same blueprint you'll find in this book.

Throughout my career in local branding, the relationships I've developed have been quite diverse, yet always a true source of joy. You see, another nugget you may not know about yours truly is that I've sat down with everyone from the CEO of a community bank to the owner of the cigar shop on the corner—sometimes in the same afternoon. I've presented branding strategies in glass-walled boardrooms with catered lunches and in back rooms that smelled like fryer oil. (BTW…the latter usually sparks the most creative ideas, not to mention the best 'eats'!)

That's the beauty of local branding—it's personal, adaptable, and built on real human connection.

Whether you're a corporate leader, startup founder, or marketing beginner, this book will help you clarify your message, strengthen your visual identity, and build brand equity in a crowded market.

At BrandVision Marketing, we've spent decades helping organizations position themselves for impact and profitability. Branding isn't about logos, taglines and color schemes alone—it's about strategy, trust, and relevance. And when done right, it's the single most powerful tool in your business arsenal.

Why?

Because a finely tuned brand identity gives consumers a trusted 'go-to' in the decision-making process. Decisions become easy and routine. And let's face it: Consumers love that! As will you when your brand emerges front and center as the beneficiary of those loyal decisions. So, let's go…

"For Mom and Dad—

Janet & Larry Trueblood…

who taught me the value of relationships, and that

love and connection outlast everything else.

I love and miss you both so much!"

1

Chapter 1: What Is a Brand, Really?

A brand is more than a logo, a clever color scheme, or a slogan your cousin thought up after "two very inspirational glasses of muscato." It's more than the image people see when they think about your company — it's the emotional and psychological relationship customers have with your business.

To you, your brand is about **reputation**. To the consumer, your brand is about **relationship**. It's a shortcut. A trust signal. A reason to choose your business over another without conducting a full background check. It's about making buying decisions easier and connecting in a way that transcends the standard customer-business dynamic.

Think of your brand as one of thousands and thousands manila folders stored in a figurative filing cabinet of the consumer's mind. Each interaction with your brand...touchpoint by touchpoint...prompts the consumer to lift out that manila folder with your brand's name on its tab. Then, they simply store new information based on that interaction before filing it away once again. Some experiences will be great (hopefully lots), some neutral (no harm there), and yes, occasionally a negative one will sneak in. It happens.

The thicker that folder is — and the more of it fills with positive interactions — the more likely your community sees you as a trusted, go-to brand. In other words, the more brand equity builds with good vibes flowing throughout.

Branding, then, is the deliberate effort to shape, guide, and nurture that relationship. The closer the distance between perception and reality for your brand in your customers' minds, the stronger that relationship will be at every future touchpoint.

The Real Battle of the Brands

Make no mistake — the real battle for your brand isn't fought on store shelves, in a loyalty club, or at the local high school gym where your sponsorship banner hangs. Those all matter, sure, but the **true** fight is in the minds of the people you serve.

It's often said that "being first" is the most important factor in marketing. I'd agree — but I'd take it further: Being **first in the mind** is the most important factor in building a successful brand.

After all, there are plenty of "first to market" examples that fizzled in the long run:

> ➢ DuMont invented the first television set in 1938.
> ➢ Hurley was first to market with a washing machine in 1907.
> ➢ The first automobile to market? Duryea in 1893.

Now, I bought a TV a few years ago and DuMont was not in the running for my dollars. It's been a while since I purchased a washing machine, but there is not a Hurley sitting in my laundry room. And Duryea? I wonder if they make a hybrid. No? Well, it's because they do not make anything anymore.

Why didn't they last?

Quite possibly because they never won the battle for **mindshare**.

It's true. The consumer's mind is a tricky place to conquer. It's crowded in there—a distinctly congested and quirky place. Further, the consumer's mind is often very irrational and challenges are many...from a marketing perspective alone. And once a position is claimed by another brand, it's hard to unseat it. But conquering the consumer's mind is one of...if not the...most important components to winning the branding game.

An Example from the Local Front

A local utilities provider — well-known for electric, gas, and water — decided to start offering fiber internet. Their reasoning was two-fold.

Well, first...the city is wired, so why not?

Okay. I get that.

But the second reason is where it all went bad. That was: "Everyone knows us! We'll use that name recognition to dominate the fiber market, too!"

On paper, it made sense. In reality? Not so much.

Why? Because in the consumer's mind lives a practical reality of wanton segmentation. This company owned "utilities" in the consumer's mind— not "communications" or "internet." Jumping from "water and gas" to "fiber internet" required a mental leap the public was simply not ready to make.

The result? Tons spent in advertising to jumpstart adoption… but they'll need to spend much more to gain any serious traction or market share.

A better approach? Launch a brand extension with a name the consumer could instantly connect to "fiber internet" — while still leveraging the parent brand's trust. This would even allow them to capitalize on the 'local' position in the consumer's mind, one that is often quite advantageous.

The lesson is simple: You win by claiming the right position in the mind. Just ask Hurley, Duryea, or DuMont — if you can find them.

The Three Must-Haves of a Strong Brand

At BrandVision Marketing, we evaluate every brand through three lenses:

1. **Distinctiveness** – What makes you stand out in your market? Does your Unique Selling Proposition (USP) make you unforgettable, or are you blending into the "me too" crowd?

2. **Relevance** – Does your difference **matter** to the customer? You can stand out in neon green overalls, but if that's not solving a real need, it's just a fashion statement. Standing out is important, but it's vital to take it a step further: Stand out in a way that eases a Pain Point. Stand

out in a way that is culturally relevant…that means something to consumers.

3. **Continuity** – Do all your touchpoints — ads, social media, website, in-store experience — feel like they came from the same brand? Consistency builds familiarity. Does the brand have the same look, feel, voice, personality? Consumers are bombarded today with marketing messages. A constant change in those aspects creates possible confusion and a quick dismissal from today's busy consumer.

DISTINCTIVENESS…*Me too doesn't cut it.*

One of the first questions I ask a prospective client is about their Unique Selling Proposition. The USP is essentially a statement that clearly defines what makes your brand different from competitors. A good USP highlights a specific feature and communicates it in a way that screams 'life altering benefit' to the consumer. It yells 'my gosh what a value' from all around. All of which they can **only** find in your brand. Essentially, a USP answers the question of **why** customers should choose your brand over another-- based on those unique advantages.

"What makes your brand stand out?"

Quite often, when asking a prospect about their USP, one answer is prominent:

"Customer service! We offer great customer service."

That's nice. But here's the thing — no one is out there bragging about their **mediocre** customer service. If everyone says they have "great" service, no one is actually saying anything.

So, the task becomes relaying that distinction in a way that 'says it…without saying it!'

One of my early agency clients was a men's wear store. They sold high-end men's wear competing against national department stores and a sea of local retailers.

Their USP? It was, indeed, service. But we had to ramp up the game. Their customer service was not the kind you just talk about. It was the kind you prove.

First, realize that these were high-end suits and upscale casual wear for the fellas. The specific clothing brands helped with the sale for the fashionista prospects, but we needed more to stand out in the competitive local landscape. We created a program where sales reps would bring the store to the client — complete with clothing options matched to the customer's style, size, and needs. No one else in the area was doing that. Suddenly, they weren't just selling suits — they were selling **time, convenience, and status**. Their USP screamed 'customer service' without ever uttering either word.

RELEVANCE…*It has to matter!*

Standing out is only half the battle. If your difference doesn't matter to the customer, you've built a very unique… waste of time.

For the men's wear store, their distinction mattered deeply to their ideal customer — busy professionals who valued their time as much as their wardrobe. Relevance made the USP stick.

Therefore, you must stand out in a way that matters to people. In a way that is truly culturally relevant to them— so they view your brand as ripe with impact for their lives.

CONTINUITY...*Speak with one brand voice.*

Brands get themselves in trouble when they change core elements on a whim.

"I'm tired of our colors."

"I woke up with a new tagline idea!"

"I'm sick of our logo."

I get it — you see this stuff every day... ad nauseam. So, yes...it's easy for you to get tired of it, if not downright sick of it! But here's the problem: by the time **you're** tired of your branding, the market is just starting to recognize it. Changing it too soon means starting over in the consumer's mind — and that's expensive.

True continuity means that whether someone sees your Facebook ad, your billboard, or your packaging, they instantly know it's **you**.

Touchpoint to touchpoint...make sure your brand resonates with a similar look, feel, structure, voice, and personality...not to mention color scheme, tagline, etc.

A consumer should be able to identify one of your ads without the logo in the ad at all. Because so many of the other elements are the same: fonts, headline continuity, sub-headline continuity, color and so much more.

Let's look at some of the Key Elements of a Brand to be mindful of:

Key Elements of a Brand

- **Purpose** – Why your business exists beyond profit.
- **Vision** – Where your brand is going long-term.
- **Mission** – How you get there every day.
- **Values** – The principles that guide your behavior.
- **Positioning** – What makes you different in your market.
- **Personality** – The tone and style of your communication.
- **Promise** – What your audience can always expect from you.

These elements work together to give your audience a sense of identity, consistency, and reliability—all crucial for trust-building. The more that trust resonates, the stronger the relationship…the stronger the brand.

Why Branding Matters

"…conversations about the marketing of brands tend to focus on hair-splitting distinctions between fairly good products. We often forget that, without this assurance of quality, there simply isn't enough trust for markets to function at all, which means that perfectly good ideas fail."
– Rory Sutherland

If you've been in business locally for a while, you've probably heard this one: "We don't advertise." Or, "we don't market ourselves."

That is, essentially the brand they wish to push—that they are above the marketing process somehow.

Spoiler alert—they do market themselves. They hand out business cards at the Chamber breakfast. They have a website that may or may not have been updated in the last decade. They sponsor the Little League team. But they skip the work of actually building a brand—because they see it as an expense instead of an investment.

But here's the problem: susceptibility.

When your business doesn't truly **stand for something** in your local market, you become just another option in a sea of "also-rans." People will choose based on a sale or price, convenience…and none of those are sustainable.

I like the metaphor of a brand being like a moat. When you think of a moat, one's mind immediately turns to medieval times and those water-filled trenches that surround the castle. Those moats were designed to keep enemies at bay while strengthening the castle's stronghold.

The same is true in business.

Picture your business like a Main Street landmark surrounded by a protective trench. That moat keeps competitors from storming your customer base, even when they launch flashy ads or undercut your pricing.

Locally, your moat could be built on:

- A network of loyal customers who recommend you to the point of advocacy.
- A community reputation earned through decades of service.
- A brand identity that instantly tells people, "This is **the** place" for what I need.

When done right, a strong brand becomes the deep moat that protects your position in the market. It's why people will drive past three other BBQ joints to get to **your** ribs… or why they'll wait for your next available appointment even if a competitor can fit them in tomorrow.

The answer to the question of "Why does Branding matter" is obvious to any company that has a distinctive, relevant brand in their market. It's less obvious when your company doesn't truly 'stand for' anything in the consumer's mind. Or when they really don't know enough about you compared to companies that have earned familiarity over the years.

Think of it like your favorite local diner—you know, the one where they start pouring your coffee before you've taken off your coat, and the waitress has already put in your "usual" without asking. That's the power of branding. I've got places like that. We all do. My movie theatre knows me so well that as soon as I walk in the door, I hear "Get Scott's cheese sticks ready!"

It's that familiarity, trust, and relationship all rolled into one that resonates. It makes you the default choice without people even checking the competition.

So, how do you dig a moat that deep? It starts with knowing exactly what you stand for, saying it consistently, and making sure every touchpoint—ads, social posts, signage, sponsorships—reinforces that same promise.

Here's why branding is your most powerful moat in your local market:

- **Differentiation:** In saturated markets, branding helps you stand out. A meaningful distinction for your brand is a first step toward a lasting relationship with the consumer.
- **Trust:** Consistent, clear branding builds credibility. Trust is huge to today's bombarded consumer. When garnered, it's often a rare commodity that leads to…
- **Loyalty:** Take a dash of Trust and combine it with a pinch of Loyalty and a profitable brand quickly follows. People connect emotionally with brands that reflect their values…over and over again.
- **Perceived Value:** A strong brand can command premium pricing. When consumers know what to expect from your brand, that trust can be seen at the cash register. In other words, it's worth the extra couple bucks to get something you know you can count on.
- **Internal Alignment:** Branding unifies your team around shared purpose and voice. Your employees are your brand's ambassadors. They literally breathe life into your brand, making it come alive. Giving them the playbook to living your brand truly ensures that your customers experience the brand in the way you intend.

All of this ultimately points to these last words from Mr. Sutherland: "Branding isn't just something to add to great products-it's essential to their very existence."

In short, a well-built local brand is like that hometown diner—once people know you, trust you, and feel connected to you, they'll keep coming back no matter who else opens up down the street. And that's exactly the kind of moat we're going to dig together in the chapters ahead.

Examples of Great Branding...with a Local Twist

We often point to Apple, Nike, or Coca-Cola when talking about branding, and for good reason. They rock! Each, in its own category is a shining beacon in the branding landscape. But let's be real—most local businesses don't have gazillion-dollar budgets or Madison Avenue ad firms on retainer. The lessons, however, are still incredibly relevant...if you know how to translate them to Main Street.

- **Apple**: Innovation, simplicity, premium quality.

  Apple is all about sleek design and making life simpler. Now, if you're running a local **HVAC company** that might look like clear, easy-to-understand service packages with zero fine print. If you're a boutique **coffee shop**, it might be offering a simple, friction-free mobile ordering system that feels intuitive. Apple's real lesson for us on the local level? Remove friction and make the customer feel smart for choosing you.

- **Nike**: Performance, aspiration, motivation.

Nike sells more than shoes—they sell the dream of pushing yourself further. A local **fitness studio** or **youth sports league** can borrow that playbook by telling stories of real community members hitting milestones. Showcase Sally who ran her first 5K at 60 years old or the local basketball team that made the playoffs. Nike's real lesson? Make your audience the hero of the story, not your business.

- **Coca-Cola**: Happiness, nostalgia, global reach.

  Coke doesn't just sell soda—it sells the feeling of sharing a moment with friends and family. For a **local diner** or family-owned **bakery**, that might mean leaning into the "memories" angle—Grandma Daisy's recipe, decades of serving the community, or even photos of multi-generational customers at the counter. Coca-Cola's real lesson? Create traditions that people can count on and further…emotionally tie those back to your business.

The Bottom Line: You don't need to be Apple, Nike, or Coca-Cola. What you need is to adopt the principles behind their branding—simplicity, aspiration, and emotional connection—and apply them in ways that resonate locally. When you do that, you carve out a spot in the consumer's mind and, more importantly, in their heart.

A Local Cautionary Tale or Two…

Now, here's what **not** to do when studying the big brands:

➢ Domino's Pizza built a national brand by burning one concept…and word…into the consumer's mind: **Delivery!** Before 'bringing food to your doorstep' was a common thing, Domino's built an entire brand around it. A local pizzeria decided to mimic that offer to keep up: "30 Minutes or Less or It's Free." Bold move. The problem? They had a limited number of drivers (all with questionable GPS skills). Long story short? They gave away too many free pizzas and in no time it wasn't just the sauce that was red.

The Takeaway? Copying the slogan of a big brand without the **infrastructure** of a big brand is a recipe for disaster (pun intended). Create your own distinction!

➢ Owning the 'luxury' position in any category is a great plus. Upscale clientele. Higher margins. Prestige. It all sounds like a winner. Right? Well, maybe. A small boutique once decided to "go luxury" in an effort to brand similarly to Tiffany & Co. or Nordstrom with an uptick in profit margins very much in sight. They rebranded with an elegant new logo, switched to black-and-gold signage, and doubled their prices. The problem? They left out the most important part of luxury branding—the **experience**.

Shoppers expected champagne-level service. However, that was not what they experienced. Instead, they got the same paper bags and distracted clerks 'ho-humming' to their social media feeds behind the counter. Far from prestige, the rebrand left people confused and, well quite annoyed. It didn't take long for foot traffic to drop—prompting a return to their old pricing. Meanwhile, the ole hit to their reputation lingered on the brand.

The Takeaway? You can't just **look** luxury—you have to **live** it at every touchpoint. If your branding promises a premium experience, everything from customer service to packaging to follow-up must deliver on that promise. Otherwise, you've donned the tuxedo jacket but matched it with board shorts.

From Inspiration to Strategy

Learning from these giants is valuable, but here's the catch: inspiration without execution is just wishful thinking. The real challenge—and opportunity—for local businesses is turning those branding principles into a clear, actionable plan that works in your community. That's where **strategy** comes in.

Conclusion

Before you invest in websites, ads, or social media, make sure your brand foundation is clear. Know who you are, who you're for, and what promise you deliver. The rest of your marketing will be exponentially more effective and a profitable brand will begin to form.

In the next chapter, we'll break down what a brand strategy actually is, why it matters, and how you can create one that's not only distinctive but also deeply rooted in your local market. Because without a strategy, even the best branding ideas risk becoming just another "good intention" filed away in that crowded manila folder in the consumer's mind.

2

Chapter 2: Brand Strategy—Define Before You Design

Brand strategy is the backbone of effective branding. It's the blueprint that guides your visual identity, your brand's personality and tone of voice, marketing, and even business decisions. Because remember, great brands align with the overall business mission and principles.

Strategy is truly step one. Think of strategy as Mission Control. Without it, your brand is like Apollo 11 blasting off in a random direction—sure, it might look flashy and even grab a few headlines along the way, but it won't land where you want it to. If you're looking for a big-time moon landing, this "one small step…" reminds us that without strategy, your brand risks being inconsistent, forgettable, or misunderstood.

What Is Brand Strategy?

A brand strategy is a long-term plan for how your brand will achieve specific goals, connect with the right audience, and differentiate itself in the market. It sets the direction for how you communicate, look, and act.

At BrandVision Marketing, we call this phase **BrandFOCUS**.

As I put on my consultant's hat day after day, I am constantly asked, "What do you think of this?"

The answer is simple: It does not matter what I think.

What does matter is what your **customers** think. Therefore, **BrandFOCUS** is essentially, the research phase in which we identify what the brand does, can or should stand for in the mind of the consumer and develop a direction for it to do exactly that. In other words…create a strategic direction to move the brand forward. How? We simply ask those that matter most: existing customers who have a standing relationship with the brand. Or, if it's a startup, we ask those who would comprise the best-fit target audience for the newbie.

Honestly, it's one of my favorite parts of the process because we are basically starting with a clean slate. Even if a brand has been around for a decade, this is a new **jumping off** point.

Before we walk through some examples, let's look at the elements we try to uncover through this process:

Key Components of a Brand Strategy:

1. **Audience Definition**
   o   Who are you trying to reach?
   o   What are their general needs, behaviors, and preferences?
   o   What are their specific Pain Points? How do you address them presently? How can you better address them?
   o   Remember, you're not typically selling to 10 million people in local market campaigns—you're selling to thousands…any number of

whom you may run into at the grocery store. Get to know them and how you can best help them.

2. **Competitive Positioning**
   - Who are your competitors?
   - What makes your brand uniquely valuable? How is your brand distinct compared to competitors? What is your Unique Selling Proposition?
   - How is your distinction relevant to your audience? Does that relevance resonate?

3. **Brand Purpose & Mission**
   - Why do you exist, and what do you stand for?
   - What is the function of your brand? What is the deeper purpose beyond that function? (e.g. a HVAC brand's function is to keep home climates cool in summer and cozy in winter, but their deeper purpose involves creating home environments where families can connect and thrive comfortably together)

4. **Core Messaging & Voice**
   - What tone and language reflect your brand's personality? The more strongly you're able to personify the brand, the more relatable it becomes to the consumer.
   - What core messages will you consistently reinforce?
   - Does your tagline and other branding elements reinforce those messages distinctly?

5. **Visual Identity Direction**
   - What colors, typography, and imagery align with your values and appeal to your audience?

6. **Goals & Metrics**
   o What does success look like, and how will you measure it? Set clearly defined goals.
   o Do not get caught up in vanity metrics. Gauge the numbers that matter.
   o Sales will sustain your brand, but what metrics help you boost those figures?

Each component offers valuable insight into a profitable direction for your brand. Understanding your audience…knowing your competition…pushing forward with a distinct purpose and mission—all of these matter in developing a strategy to connect with and present a brand that bears differentiation and relevance in the local market.

Exempli Gratia of BrandFOCUS…

Let's go through some examples of the strategic formation phase of the branding process. As mentioned, at BrandVision Marketing, we call it **BrandFOCUS**.

This is the research phase when we identify a profitable direction to take the brand.

Sometimes it involves coordinating multiple Focus Groups with a mixture of current and prospective customers. Sometimes, it involves online surveys. Other times we utilize one-on-one personal interviews if the topic is deeply personal. Sometimes it's a combination of two or more.

Regardless of the tool, it involves a deep dive into the thinking process and relational aspects of the customer with the specific brand or category.

AFTER-SCHOOL CARE...*Is it really about Safety or Guilt?*

BrandVision Marketing worked with an after-school care provider with one goal: Develop a waiting list for their post-school day care services for kids K-5. The new owner was ready for a re-brand from a tired and basic concept, but he felt as if an emphasis on safety was the direction to take the brand. After all, every parent needs to know their child is going into a safe and healthy environment right?

Made sense, certainly, but we conducted a series of focus groups to confirm the notion's validity.

Guess what?

After five focus groups with more than 60 participants, we discovered a new direction entirely.

What we discovered is that parents overwhelmingly expected the after school care to be a safe and positive environment. That was a 'no-brainer' which leveled the playing field. Their main Pain Point, however? It was guilt. What we discovered is that they hated working through that part of the day and having to use **any** after school provider. Period. However, if they picked up little Johnny and he was having a blast? If little Chrissy was begging to stay for another hour? Well, that sense of fun their kids experienced greatly alleviated any and all guilt from the equation. And the parent then felt much better about everything!

So, we created a school mascot...a positively, playful and only slightly pernicious pelican to center the branding around. With T-Shirts, Posters, Ads and more, we shared a great vision of what parents could expect from the brand.

Within two months, the client had a waiting list and we had a happy client.

The takeaway? Don't stop at the obvious (safety). Dig deeper into the real Pain Points your audience feels and address them. Remember the value of relevance!

COMMUNITY BANK..._It's about connection. It's about relationship._

BrandVision Marketing has worked with numerous financial institutions, mainly community banks and credit unions. Like most categories, these institutions fit that all-important model of grounding the brand in relationship. This is true especially since they are handling something of great value to their customers: their money!

When working with a new community bank in the area. They were facing stiff competition from numerous community banks, regional and national banks and credit unions. We conducted a series of focus groups to identify a strategic direction that would help them stand out from intense rivals.

What we heard repeatedly was stories of bank employees going the extra mile, "I'll see Peggy from the bank at the convenient store on my way to work—I'm running behind and don't have time to drop in, but I tell her what I need and it's taken care of...time and time again!"

Telling the brand experience through those stories...along with adopting the tagline of "We can take care of that!" became a core part of a strategy for a bank that soared from $10m in deposits to $270m+ in record time.

The takeaway? Your USP (Unique Selling Proposition) may already live in your stories—it just needs to be told well and consistently.

ATTORNEY/PERSONAL INJURY...*Testimonials setting the tone.*

The legal category has always been a favorite of mine because it's a challenging sector to brand. You see, no one 'wants' to hire an attorney. They simply 'must' hire one. So, building a legal brand means that formula of distinction, relevance and continuity is a toughy.

Sure, attorneys get teased for wild ads using nicknames like 'The Hammer' or 'The Bulldog,' but that noise leaves a lot of room for firms who want to brand themselves differently—as authentic, trustworthy, and responsive. That was the case with one particular personal injury attorney.

BrandVision Marketing worked with a personal injury firm that had been around for ten years and held a very solid reputation in the market. But they needed to grow and needed a stable, consistent flow of clients to make that happen.

During **BrandFOCUS** we conducted numerous personal interviews with former clients to learn more about what was at the heart of their connection with the firm. We learned that it was grounded in responsiveness, doing what you said you would do, setting reasonable expectations and protection--truly fighting on their behalf...after all, these were individuals who needed someone standing up for them. This firm did. Time and time again. It all led to very strong relationships.

Further, once we stabilized their program with a series of testimonials that showcased the brand experience, we brought in a local sports celebrity to serve as a spokesperson, sparking relevance in a category that struggled in that department. From there, the brand soared to new heights with new case files reaching records year after year.

The takeaway? In tough categories, credibility often comes from the voices of those you've already helped—not just from shouting louder than the competition.

What about the other guy?

Ahh, yes. The other guy—the competitor. Sometimes friendly, sometimes hostile, but always lurking like that car in your rearview mirror that looks way closer than it really is. Why? Because it always **feels** like they are hot on your tails.

Spoiler alert: that's where your brand comes in. And, that is why this part of the process is so important. It's this phase where your brand serves as a machete, clearing the path forward, carving out distinction and relevance so you're not fighting shoulder-to-shoulder in the same crowded lane.

The goal is simple. The execution is far more challenging. Your goal is to find your own "blue ocean" instead of wading into a bloody river of sameness. And that begins with learning about the other guy.

Assessing the competition is a critical component of your brand strategy—and it requires brutal honesty. So, take off those {YOUR BRAND}-colored glasses and look at things objectively from the consumer's point of view. Visit their websites. Stake out their social media. Do a little Mystery Shopping--walk into their locations to learn more about their sales process. Call their customer service line to gain insight into that aspect. Remember, you're not just checking boxes here—rather, you are in pure discovery mode. You are discovering what **they** own in the mind of your shared customer, and where your opportunity lies.

Here are some questions to guide your assessment:

- **Strengths & Weaknesses**: What do they do exceptionally well? Where do they come up short? (Look at both their business **operations** and their brand **presence** because there may be ways to build your own brand around a specific 'operations' function/feature that greatly benefits your market and helps you carve out differentiation)
- **Positioning**: Positioning is identifying a uniquely favorable perception versus a competing brand. Examine what the competition **stands for** in the eyes of the consumer. Is their distinction clear—or are they blending into the crowd?
- **Relevance**: Why does what they stand for actually matter to the local consumer? (This one often separates the leaders from the "me-toos.")
- **Brand Elements**: What is their look, feel, and tone? What is their brand's personality? Voice? Take note of color schemes, taglines, typography, and messaging style. Is there good continuity from touchpoint to touchpoint?

- **Geographic Reach**: What is their Area of Dominant Influence (ADI)? Do they dominate across the market or mostly pull from a few miles around their location?
- **Resources**: Do they have deep pockets to defend their turf, and market share, or limited resources?

With these answers in tow, look for gaps—places where competitors are either weak, irrelevant, or absent altogether. Those gaps? They are opportunities. That's where your brand should live, grow, and own.

Cutting a New Path...

Assessing your competition isn't just about finding weaknesses—it's about spotting the gaps where you can shine. Think of it this way: you don't have to outspend or outscale the "other guy." You just have to carve out a space that matters to your audience. Here are three lessons from Main Street businesses that did just that:

The Local Hardware Store vs. The Big-Box Giants

A family-owned hardware store found themselves staring down Lowe's and Home Depot. Compete on price or selection? Nope! That was a losing battle. So instead, they built their brand around **being the neighbor who knows**. Their moat was trust and personal service—the kind of advice and solutions that can't be 'big-boxed'! The big boys may talk that game but they do not live it. It doesn't take too many trips through the big boy's doors with your questions at the ready and answers with the crickets! That spelled opportunity for a brand hell-bent on helping—with knowledge, expertise and going the extra mile.

The Local Gym vs. National Fitness Chains

While nationally recognized, franchise gyms sold cheap memberships, one boutique studio doubled down on **community**, **relationship** and **accountability**. They created an atmosphere where skipping class meant your friends noticed. Their brand wasn't about "access to equipment 24/7"—no, it was about belonging, results, and connection. And that was something much harder for the chains to replicate.

The Independent Bookstore vs. Amazon

Amazon may own selection and convenience, but a local bookstore built their moat around **experience**. Curated staff picks, handwritten notes tucked in books, Kids' Storytime, and events with local authors created a reason to visit. Rather than trying to emulate the ole everything to everyone—they just needed to be something special to their community. Replicating the good old fashion community thriving bookstore grounded in customer experience and relationship.

The takeaway?

You don't need to copy competitors—or beat them at their own game. Instead, build your moat where they are weakest. Compete on **meaning**, not on size. That's how local brands win.

A local coffee shop in one of our markets found itself directly across the street from—you guessed it—Seattle's own version of the 'Ma & Pa' killer...Starbucks. (Hey! I'm just joshin' because I love their Iced Chai Latte!) On paper, it looked like a death sentence. Starbucks had the brand recognition, the marketing muscle, and the drive-thru line that seemed to wrap around the whole city.

Instead of trying to beat Starbucks at its own game (speed, convenience, ubiquity), this shop picked up the branding machete and cut a different path. They leaned into what Starbucks **could not** replicate: local connection. They became the "community living room coffee shop". They hosted open mic nights...featured local artists on the walls...offered that first name service that screamed relationship. In short, they maneuvered quickly in ways the corporate giant just could not, all while embracing their local roots.

Within a year, they weren't gasping for air. Far from it— they had lines of their own. They owned "warmth, community, and belonging" in the consumer's mind, while Starbucks remained "fast coffee." Both had moats. Both had loyal customers. But the local shop carved out distinction and brought relevance that mattered deeply to **their** audience and built a successful brand in the process.

That's the power of assessing your competition honestly. Once you see where they are strong, you can decide where you don't need to fight—and where you can win by being different. And **that**, my friend, puts you ahead of the game.

Developing Your Brand Positioning Statement

The end goal with our research component, **Brand**FOCUS is to develop a Brand Positioning Statement that is concise and clarifies who you help, how you help them, and why it matters. It serves to give you a productively profitable direction to take the brand because you have been able to identify two key things: 1) what matters to those who matter most (e.g. those who have interacted with the brand and love it) and, 2) what matters to people in your category in general.

Further, the process should give you a clear-cut path forward by honestly assessing where you stand among your competition. This helps you wield that machete to carve out your own profitable path apart from the other guy.

Below is the format we use for the Brand Positioning Statement. Just plug in what you have learned from your own research and begin to see a strategic direction take shape.

Brand Positioning Statement Example Format:

For [Target Audience], [Your Brand] is the [Category] that [Unique Value or Distinctive Benefit] because [Reason to Believe].

Brand Positioning Statement Example:

For personal injury attorneys, BrandVision Marketing is the strategic branding agency that identifies a profitable brand direction and then implements an extensive marketing plan to bring the brand to life, building trust and market presence through focused creativity.

The Brand Strategy Process

1. **Research:** At BrandVision Marketing, we call it BrandFOCUS. It's the deep dive stage where you ask your loyal customers why they have connected with your brand. Use any number of research tools-- Focus Groups, Customer Interviews, Surveys (in-person or online, if the situation fits). Look at competitor analysis to learn more about their positioning and where you can find a profitable niche.
2. **Strategy Development:** Craft messaging pillars, positioning, and brand story to provide you with a productive and profitable brand direction.
3. **Discovery Workshops & Documentation:** Align team perspectives on brand mission, values, and vision. Create a brand strategy guide for team-wide consistency. At BrandVision Marketing, we call it the *Brand Guideline Book*. More on this in an upcoming chapter but suffice it to say 'getting everyone on the same page' to make the brand come to life is vital. This step we refer to as BrandTRAINING.
4. **Validation:** Test concepts with real users for feedback.

5. **Communication Plan:** We call this the **Brand**PLAN. It's time to take the word to Main Street and let prospects know what you're all about.

Uh-Oh...Common Mistakes to Avoid

- **Designing a logo before defining your audience**…I get it! Logos are fun. They make your concept a tangible reality, right! And yes, it's tempting to rush to the fun part—colors, fonts, a shiny new logo. But a logo without a defined audience is just decoration. If you don't know who you're speaking to, the visual identity will lack meaning. For example, a playful, cartoon-style logo may resonate in a children's boutique, but the same design would undermine credibility for a healthcare provider. We've used **Brand**FOCUS to test logos with the target audience. Don't be afraid to take a few ideas to test with your audience! *Remember: Audience first, visuals second.*
- **Using buzzwords with no real clarity**… How many times have you seen "cutting-edge solutions" or "world-class service"? These phrases may sound impressive in the boardroom, but they don't anchor a brand in anything real. Buzzwords without substance create noise, not distinction. Instead, brands need clear, relatable language that aligns with what the customer actually values—whether that's convenience, trust, affordability, or expertise. *Remember: Use your words—and make them relevant!*
- **Copying competitors instead of differentiating**… It's natural to peek at what competitors are doing, but building your brand by imitation is a dead end.

If you look, sound, and act just like the other guy, you've given the consumer no reason to pick you. You've created no discernable brand at all. Remember, branding is about creating a distinct position in the consumer's mind. Your task is not to blend in—it's to carve out a space that only your brand can own. *Remember: Use your machete to carve your own path!*

- **Having too many messages that confuse rather than clarify**… If you're everything to everyone, you end up being nothing to anyone. Mixed messages leave customers guessing about what you stand for. Effective branding requires consistency—touchpoint to touchpoint, campaign to campaign. A clear core message repeated often builds recognition, trust, and memorability. Confusion, on the other hand, only garners you a dismissal and drives people toward a competitor who communicates more clearly. *Remember: Stay on point…and make your point meaningful and clear.*

Conclusion

Great brands don't happen by accident. They are built on strategy—rooted in purpose and guided by insight. They grow in value the more deeply they resonate with your market; and then…the thicker that manila folder of the mind becomes. By defining your brand by learning more from those who engage with it, you create a brand that resonates deeply, performs better, and grows sustainably.

With a strategic direction in place, it's time to give your brand a face, a voice, and a personality. Chapter 3 will take that blueprint and bring it to life through your brand identity—the visuals, tone, and vibe that make your strategy tangible in the marketplace. This is where your audience stops just hearing about your brand and starts experiencing it.

Chapter 3: Building a Brand Identity that Connects

Your brand identity is the outward expression of your brand strategy. It's the "face" of your business—the look, feel, sound, and vibe that customers encounter every time they interact with you. All of those components blend to set the tone for their brand experience.

That tone is important. It's often your first impression. It serves to **say** so many of the right things for your brand as consumers start a new manila folder of the mind bearing your name.

Done right? That's good news! Then, your identity becomes recognizable, trustworthy, and emotionally engaging. It's the first step toward giving your brand a personality…a voice that resonates with Main Street and beyond. Done correctly and your brand identity distinguishes you from everyone else and does so in a way that truly matters.

Done poorly? Uh-oh…bad news. Then, it confuses customers, weakens trust, and makes you blend into the background of your local market. It sets a negative tone for what you stand for in your community. Even worse…if unprofessional, probably sends your brand on the exact opposite path of the productively profitable existence you are hoping it achieves. You're easily dismissed. You're not taken seriously versus the competition. All in all, you find yourself in a place where success stagnates, and an annoying plug stops up that once hopeful flow of cash.

Brand identity isn't just design fluff. It is **strategy** brought to life through colors, fonts, imagery, and voice. In fact, brand identity is one of the most powerful tools a local business has to shape perception and create consistency in the consumer's mind.

Going through the research steps from the last chapter helped you identify a profitable direction to begin this journey. Now, what you learned is ready to spring into action, breathing life into your brand.

Remember as you begin this design stage, people buy based on **emotional factors**. Logic? It comes in after the fact to justify or rationalize the purchase. Make sure you are tapping into those emotional aspects that you identified during the research phase.

Again and for emphasis: **Brand identity is the outward expression of your brand strategy**. This is where the rubber begins to jive with the road.

Let's start by looking at the various components of your brand's identity. There are seven main elements that come together to create a strong, consistent identity:

What Makes Up Brand Identity?

1. **Logo** – A mark or symbol representing your business
2. **Tagline** – A short sentence that defines the brand experience for your customer

3. **Color Palette** A set of brand colors that evoke emotion and create cohesion
4. **Typography** – Fonts that reflect your brand's tone and function across media
5. **Imagery Style** – Photography, illustrations, and graphics that tell your brand story
6. **Voice and Tone** – The consistent language and attitude used across all brand messaging
7. **Design System** – A style guide to ensure brand consistency across platforms

Now, let's look at each of these branding elements more closely.

Logo – A mark or symbol representing your business. For a local brand, your logo doesn't have to be complicated—it has to be memorable.

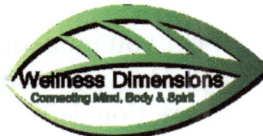

A family-owned diner may use a hand-drawn illustration of the founder's first menu item. A local gym may include an icon of a landmark (think: a bridge, skyline, or mascot) that grounds it in the community. But the imagery should set the tone for the brand's identity—bringing personality, voice and so much more together in one symbolic nest. The previous page contains a few of the logos that we have created over the last 30+ years.

Tagline –One of my favorite brand elements is the tagline. A tagline is a short phrase—usually seven words or less— that defines the brand experience for the consumer. Think of it as your brand's promise boiled down to its essence. A strong tagline separates you from the pack, communicates your personality, and makes your brand more memorable.

It's amazing to me how many businesses have shelved this tool altogether. Yet, history proves the power of a good one. When you hear:

> ➢ "Just Do It."
> ➢ "The Quicker-Picker-Upper."
> ➢ "Finger Lickin' Good."

…I bet you immediately thought of Nike, Bounty, and KFC. That's the magic of a tagline—clarity, memorability, and emotion delivered in just a few words.

The Arguments Against Taglines (And My Take)

Some in the marketing spectrum argue that taglines aren't worth the effort. Common objections include:

> ➢ Taglines have a short shelf life

> ➤ With consumers on smaller screens and limited digital ad space, taglines take up too much valuable 'real estate'
> ➤ Taglines are given too much responsibility
> ➤ A tagline may not be needed considering your brand name

I'll freely admit—there is **some** truth in two of these. Yes, digital ads don't leave much room, but that doesn't mean you ditch a tagline entirely. Just don't use it **everywhere**. And yes, a strong name can carry a lot of weight, but most names don't clearly position a business against competitors. That's where a tagline fills the gap.

The other objections? That's where I say, "Grab your ears and pull your head out." A tagline shouldn't have a short shelf life if it reflects your brand's core promise—something that rarely changes. If you're swapping it every six months because you're "bored," that's not strategy; that's chaos. I once worked with a credit union whose president changed the tagline nine times in a single year just because he "thought up a new one." That kind of inconsistency doesn't build brand equity—it confuses people.

As for the claim that a tagline carries "too much responsibility"—well, only if it is poorly written. A good tagline isn't a brand biography. It's a positioning statement: distinct, succinct, and relevant.

Why You Should Use a Tagline

When done right, a tagline communicates three powerful things in one punch:

✓ Your personality (playful? serious? aspirational?).

✓ The scope of what you do.
✓ Your unique selling proposition (why choose you instead of the other guy?).

That's why taglines remain one of the most underutilized—but most valuable—branding tools. They give consumers a shorthand way to remember you, repeat you, and recommend you.

One of the most effective taglines BrandVision Marketing ever created came straight from our **BrandFOCUS** research. In focus groups, customers of a community bank repeatedly shared stories of employees going the extra mile—handling requests on the fly, solving problems quickly, and making banking feel personal. Out of that insight came the tagline: **"We can take care of that!"** It wasn't just a line; it was a promise people already believed. Paired with testimonial ads that echoed the phrase, it stuck in the market and became shorthand for the bank's reputation. Simple, memorable, and true.

Another example still makes me smile. A personal injury attorney we worked with adopted the tagline: **"Have you called Ralph Brown? You should!"** It was conversational, approachable, and easy to remember…not to mention speaking directly to a strong call-to-action. The moment I knew it had broken through? I was listening to a local sports talk show, and a caller jokingly said about a league dispute, "Have you called Ralph Brown? You should!" That's when you know a tagline isn't just marketing—it's part of the local conversation.

The bottom line? A great tagline isn't fluff. It offers consumers a critical, vital insight into your brand and, when it really resonates, it becomes part of the culture around you.

Of course, a tagline alone isn't enough—it has to live alongside your visuals, colors, and voice to create a cohesive identity. Let's look at how those pieces come together.

Color Palette – A set of brand colors that evoke emotion and create cohesion.

A color palette is more than just picking your "favorite" shades — it's the backbone of how your brand feels at first glance. Individual colors carry meaning and trigger emotion. A red-and-black combo sets a very different tone than a pink-and-gold pairing. Done right, your color choices match your brand's personality, stand apart from competitors, and stick in the memory of your audience.

Color is especially powerful for local branding. A children's tutoring center might lean toward bright, playful colors that spark curiosity and energy. A landscaping company using deep greens and earth tones will naturally feel aligned with growth and nature. But beware of the copycat trap: if every other landscaper in your county uses the same green-and-brown palette, you may want to zag instead of zig. Distinction matters — as long as it still aligns with your brand strategy.

Color sets tone and feeling. Remember the vitality of **emotion**. Colors really come into play with the emotive element. Different colors establish different tones, vibes, personality and much more. There is plenty of psychology behind what colors mean to consumers.

Here's a simple rundown of the psychology in play:

Red → energy, urgency, passion (fast food chains use it for a reason).

Blue → trust, reliability, calm (banks and insurance companies love it).

Green → growth, health, balance (perfect for environmental or financial brands).

Yellow → optimism, clarity, friendliness (great for family-focused brands).

Black/**Gray** → sophistication, strength, modernity (think high-end retail).

Orange → fun, creativity, enthusiasm (often used in education or entertainment).

Purple → imagination, wisdom, luxury (a strong choice when used sparingly).

These aren't "rules," mind you, but they do reflect how consumers instinctively respond. The real question is: **what do you want people to feel when they see your brand?**

A local coffee shop might lean into warm browns, cream tones, and muted greens to evoke comfort, coziness, and connection. These colors immediately suggest a welcoming space where people can gather, recharge, and feel 'right at home'. A hardware store, by contrast, might use deep reds, steel grays, and bold blacks to signal durability, strength, and reliability. In both cases, the colors reflect the brand's personality and the emotions they want to spark in their audience.

Now, imagine if that same coffee shop decided to use neon green and jet black. Instead of cozy and inviting, it might feel more like you're about to do squats and curls at a 24-hour gym. Now, when the morning 'curls' you're accustomed to involve lifting your coffee to your lips…well, it may not be the best color combo. Sure, it might wake you up—but probably not in the way you expect from your morning latte.

The same goes for the hardware store. Picture one decked out in pastel pinks and soft purples. Unless they're trying to position themselves as the world's first 'boutique spa for hammers,' it's just not the same feel. Customers would feel a disconnect between what they see and what they expect—and confusion is never a good brand strategy.

One cautionary tale: within a week, two of our clients — a credit union and a community bank — hosted big customer events with tons of swag. Except their giveaways had nothing to do with their color schemes. The "green-and-gold" bank was handing out red shirts, blue tote bags, and purple koozies. The "green-and-white" credit union was shelling out red pens, blue notepads, and teal umbrellas. When I failed to contain my **WTF face**, they shrugged and said, "We were tired of those colors."

That's when BrandVision Marketing started offering promotional products. Because here's the truth: your color scheme is not a mood swing. It's your signature. Your audience isn't tired of it — in fact, **they're counting on it to recognize your brand instantly**.

So, think ahead: will these colors work on clothing, signage, business cards, and digital platforms? Can they translate affordably onto swag and promotional items without costing you an arm and a leg in setup charges? Consistency is what builds recognition, and recognition builds trust.

Color is one of your brand's most powerful cues. Don't treat it like a trip down the paint aisle at Benjamin Moore — treat it like the emotional shorthand for everything your business stands for.

💡 Try This: A Color Walk on Main Street

Try this easy little exercise. Take a short drive or walk through your local business district. Jot down the color palettes you see most often on storefronts, signs, and logos.

- Which colors grab your attention immediately?
- Which colors feel overused or blend into the background?
- Which colors seem to "fit" the business, and which feel off-brand?

For example, I live in a college town, right? Go Vols! We're known for our distinctive shade of "Tennessee Orange", which you see many businesses trying to emulate as a way to say, 'hey folks…we're local'. That's great, but it does little to create distinction. That's why when creating my own company's color scheme; I went with Red and Black. Red to grab attention and Black to relay a sense of professionalism and stability—certainly NOT to support the rival Georgia Bulldogs (I think I just threw up a little). But you get my point, right? Your brand's selection of color scheme is one of your first opportunities to truly stand out. You simply don't do that by blending.

So, ask yourself: **If your business were added to the exercise above, would your colors help you stand out while staying true to your brand personality?**

This quick exercise not only sharpens your eye but also helps you avoid falling into the "sea of sameness" in your local market.

⌨ Try This: A Digital Color Scan

Scroll through your Facebook or Instagram feed, or spend 10 minutes browsing local business websites. Pay close attention to the colors that pop up most often.

- Do certain industries in your area lean heavily on the same color (e.g., lots of blue for banks, lots of green for landscapers)?
- Which ads or websites immediately caught your eye — and why?
- Did the color palette make the brand feel trustworthy, fun, serious, or outdated?

Then ask yourself: **If your ad appeared in this same feed tomorrow, would it stand out or blend in?**

This quick scan helps you see what your audience is seeing daily — and gives you the insight to choose colors that break through the digital noise while still feeling authentic to your brand.

💡 Tip: Test Your Colors in the Wild

Before you lock in your palette, take it for a spin. Ask yourself:

✓ Does this palette match the **emotion** I want my
   brand to spark?
✓ If my colors were a room, would people want to
   stay in it—or run out? Do they mesh and blend well
   together?
✓ Do these colors make sense **everywhere** my brand
   will live (website, advertising, social media,
   brochures, promotional products, signage, etc.)?
✓ Do they clash with competitors—or stand apart in a
   good way?

Do This…Mock up your colors on real items—like a
brochure, a t-shirt, or coffee mug. If it looks awkward or
feels out of place to you, your audience will feel it, too.

Typography – Fonts that reflect your brand's tone and
function across media.

Typography is one of those subtle brand elements people
don't consciously think about—but they **feel** it. The right
font can make your business look professional,
approachable, or completely unforgettable. The wrong font
can make you look sloppy, outdated, or even
untrustworthy.

A sleek sans-serif font (a sans serif font is a typeface that
does **not** have the small projecting features at the ends of
its letters) communicates modernity and innovation—
perfect for a local tech startup. A classic serif font suggests
tradition and stability—ideal for a community bank,
healthcare provider, insurance group, or law firm.

Also, think beyond appearance and toward functionality.
Your font family must work across the entire media

landscape—on your website, in ads, on signage, and even on promotional products. Some fonts just don't translate well outside of print. Keep it versatile and above all, legible. Legible equals functional and in the branding world, that is a win! An elegant cursive font, for instance, can feel upscale, yes. But if it's hard to read, it works against you.

Remember: if people have to **work** to read your brand, they won't.

🔊 *True Story…* Working with a community bank trying to strengthen its hometown ties, we knew their typography needed to feel bold, friendly, and welcoming. They already had their logo, but their tagline and typography needed to pave the road. The bank was known as The Home Bank and their brand resounded with relationship. They truly wanted you to feel at ease and completely comfortable in your dealings with them. The tagline was easy: "Welcome Home." The font? Cooper Black—a warm, sturdy typeface with just enough friendliness in its curves to make you feel at ease. Whether on billboards, brochures, or tote bags, "Welcome Home!" felt like more than words—it felt like a promise.

"Welcome Home!"

Font Tip #1: Choose a font hierarchy (headline, subhead, body text) and stick to it. Your audience will subconsciously thank you for the consistency. And your recognizability? Off the charts!

Font Tip #2: Stick to **two main typefaces**—one for headlines, one for body copy. Add a third only if you have a very clear purpose (like accent text or branding for a campaign). Too many fonts = visual chaos.

Typography Quick Reference Guide

Modern & Clean (Tech, Startups, Innovative Brands)

- ❖ Helvetica Neue – sleek, simple, universally recognized.
- ❖ Open Sans – versatile and great for digital readability.
- ❖ Lato – contemporary, approachable sans serif.
- ❖ Montserrat – bold, geometric, makes a strong statement online.

Traditional & Trustworthy (Banks, Law Firms, Healthcare)

- ❖ Times New Roman – classic, but can feel too common if overused.
- ❖ Georgia – professional, warm, and highly readable on screens.
- ❖ Merriweather – elegant yet practical for digital-first use.
- ❖ Baskerville – timeless, adds a touch of sophistication.

Playful & Friendly (Childcare, Cafés, Boutiques)

- ❖ Comic Neue – a modern, polished upgrade from Comic Sans.
- ❖ Poppins – rounded, clean, and cheerful.

- ❖ Baloo – fun and chunky, but still easy to read.
- ❖ Fredoka One – playful without being too childish.

Luxury & Elegant (Spas, High-End Retail, Fine Dining)

- ❖ Didot – thin, stylish, fashion-industry favorite.
- ❖ Bodoni – classic, elegant, and dramatic in headlines.
- ❖ Playfair Display – refined serif with a modern twist.
- ❖ Cinzel – formal and Roman-inspired, adds gravitas.

Imagery Style – Photography, illustrations, and graphics that tell your brand story.

You've heard the old saying, **"A picture is worth a thousand words,"** right? For your brand, it's worth even more. Imagery is one of the fastest ways to show—not just tell—what your business is all about.

For local businesses, glossy stock photos rarely cut it. They may look nice, but they don't **feel** like you. Instead, show your people, your place, and your customers. Is your brand built around connection with employees? Highlight their faces and stories. Do you want to show your community ties? Capture moments in familiar local spots—your storefront on Main Street, a well-known landmark, or the county fair.

And yes, when using customer photos: get permission. (Did I mention…**get permission?** There, now I've said it twice. No lawsuits for you.)

A boutique featuring real shoppers will feel more authentic than catalog images. A local credit union highlighting employees chatting with neighbors at the farmer's market communicates belonging. Compare that with the overused handshake stock photo—you know the one—and the difference in authenticity is night and day.

📣 *True Story*...BrandVision Marketing worked with a community bank trying to strengthen local ties. We took around employees to high profile and easily recognized landscapes in town to capture them...in those spots...interacting with the community. It's a subtle shift in imagery but certainly worked to bridge the gap with the community that they so desperately needed.

Think of your imagery as an **invitation**. When your photos feel real, warm, and rooted in the community, people don't just see your brand—they imagine themselves in it. And that's how you turn a picture into connection, helping your brand come to life.

Imagery Style Checklist

- ✓ **Local over stock:** Use real people, places, and moments whenever possible.
- ✓ **Faces over objects:** Human connection always beats staged props. Pets and Kids are winners!
- ✓ **Consistency counts:** Stick to the same filters, tones, or photo style for cohesion.
- ✓ **Root it in place:** Include recognizable community backdrops to build trust.
- ✓ **Always get permission:** (Yes, I said it again. Because you'll thank me later.)

Your imagery should be inviting, especially on the local front. Use it to connect your brand with your community and customers. Make your imagery an invitation and your brand identity will take a keen and positive step forward.

Local Hero: Photography features real baristas, latte art, and cozy community scenes. Customers feel like they belong.

Local Fail: Buying generic stock photos of models sipping coffee in sterile studios. Locals can tell "that's not our town…that's not us…that's not me!" That means a flail and fail!

Voice and Tone – The consistent language and attitude used across all brand messaging.

This is where your brand's personality really comes alive. The clearer and more human that personality feels, the easier it is for people to build a relationship with your business.

Take, for example, a community bank BrandVision Marketing worked with in Tennessee. Though it had been open three years, it struggled to stand out in a crowded county of 140,000 people and plenty of banking options. Our **Brand**FOCUS research revealed that customers appreciated the staff's warmth and helpfulness, yet the bank's external messaging came across flat—no community tie, a lack of focus and no real sense of personality.

So, we introduced an easy-going spokesperson: a soft-spoken preacher from my hometown in Indiana, a very likeable persona that served as a true connection point that personified the brand. He became the human face of the brand—a neighborly voice that felt like a brother to some, a fatherly figure to others, and a trusted friend to all. That shift gave the bank an authentic voice people could immediately recognize and trust.

The results? Total assets grew more than 47% in just three years. Proof that finding the right voice and tone doesn't just sound good—it drives growth by giving the community a brand they can genuinely relate to.

Your brand's voice and tone is an opportunity to truly personify your brand, making it something to genuinely connect with and helping fill that manila folder of the mind with wonderfully positive experiences.

Think of two local coffee shops. You walk by the first and their chalkboard reads, "Espresso yourself!" or "Mondays happen. Coffee helps." Further, their Instagram captions sound like a witty, friendly neighbor. People connect with the humor and warmth.

Next, you walk by the second and see a similar board, but it reads, "Main Street Coffee Co. is a world-class beverage delivery entity that maximizes customer satisfaction outcomes." Uhh…appetite for cappuccino officially lost, unless of course, you do an about face and walk back toward that first shop! Simply put: voice and tone matter!

Design System – A style guide to ensure brand consistency across platforms.

At BrandVision Marketing, we often joke that we're not just marketers—we're brand bodyguards. If a client needs a sign, we've got their CMYK codes ready. If the high school

yearbook ad is due tomorrow, we'll make sure it matches
their typography and tone perfectly. Everything funnels
through us so that, whether it's a billboard or a church
picnic flyer, it all feels like **them**.

But here's the thing—and put on your **surprised face** for
this one—not everyone has a BrandVision Marketing
watching their back. Instead, they've got a cousin running
social media, a nephew building the website, and a spouse
balancing the marketing budget. With so many cooks in the
kitchen, brand continuity becomes an oft mourned casualty.
Logos stretch, colors shift, voices change—and pretty soon
the brand looks more like a patchwork quilt than a trusted
identity.

That's where a **Design System** comes in. You see, split
personalities might make for good TV drama, but they
don't make for good branding. When your visuals, voice,
and messaging contradict each other, it renders your brand
dysfunctional. A Design System is your rulebook, your
blueprint, your insurance policy against chaos—your
brand's quick trip to the counselor to keep everyone on the
same page and out of dysfunction.

Take, for example, a local HVAC company. They may
know heating and cooling like the back of their coiling
systems, right? And, they may have the right idea when
investing in shirts, trucks, business cards, and ads. The
problem? If they've bypassed the ole Design System,
there's a good chance every vendor is "doing their own
thing"…at least to some extent. Trucks roam
neighborhoods wrapped in an off-brand shade of fire-
engine red with a blocky font. The technicians wear powder
blue polos with a completely stretched logo stitched on the
chest. The visuals? Well, the social media graphics look
like they were designed on a cousin's old laptop using clip

art from the 90's. And the business cards? Let's just say you'd never know they belonged to the same company. Brand continuity shot…brand damage done.

To a consumer, this is incredibly confusing. "Which company was this again?" "Are they trustworthy?" "If they can't keep their **own** brand straight, would they really keep my air conditioning working in July?"

 That's the risk. Branding isn't just about slapping a logo in the corner. It's about weaving sameness and clarity into every touchpoint so the community knows—without a doubt—who you are, what you stand for, and why you matter. In short, a design system helps you build trust one consistent impression at a time.

With the creation and implementation of a simple Design System—clear color codes, one logo with contextual variations and usage, defined fonts, and a handful of guidelines for tone—the transformation is immediate. Clarity reigns. Suddenly, the look is polished, reliable, and consistent. Customers don't have to work to recognize them, and that recognition turns quickly into trust.

A strong design system spells out:

- ✓ Color codes (RGB, CMYK, Pantone)
- ✓ Logo usage rules (yes, even what **not** to do with it)
- ✓ Typography hierarchy (headlines, subheads, body text—what font to use when)
- ✓ Photography and illustration style
- ✓ Voice and tone guidelines

Think of it as the glue that holds all your brand elements together. Without it, every piece of communication is a gamble. With it, even if your cousin is still on Instagram duty, they'll at least be playing by the same rules.

Pulling it All Together

When you look at brand identity as seven distinct elements, it's easy to think of them as separate boxes to check. But these seven elements are a **team**…one cohesive unit. Teamwork matters. Think about it—if your starting pitcher throws a shutout through eight innings, but your closer blows a 3–0 lead in the ninth…you lose! Not into sports? Okay. Try this: Luke doesn't destroy the Death Star without Han blasting Darth Vader into a tailspin. Not a Star Wars nerd like yours truly? Fine. Last try: Think of these seven as instruments in a band. A great logo might be the lead singer, but if the color palette, typography, imagery, tagline, voice, and design system aren't in harmony, the whole performance falls flat.

To see how this works in practice, let's walk through a local example. I love my hometown of Salem, Indiana. One reason why? Donuts!!! Sitting on the town square is the #3 ranked bakery in the state, but if you ask me, it's the best donut shop on the planet—H&R Bakery. Now, imagine you are opening a family-owned neighborhood bakery of your own. Let's run through the elements:

Your bakery **Logo** doesn't need to look like it belongs on the Las Vegas strip. It just needs to be memorable, simple, and true to your story. Maybe it's a rolling pin crossed with wheat stalks, forming the shape of a rising sun. That mark says "fresh," "local," and "warmth"—all in one glance.

Second? Your **tagline**. Make sure it is succinct and distinct. Seven words or less that positions you against competitors while filling your brand full of relevance like those amazing cream-filled maple-iced Long Johns. A short, punchy tagline seals the deal. Instead of something vague like "Quality You Can Taste," what about "Baked Fresh. Shared Daily." In just four words, you've captured freshness, routine, and community. That's a promise people can remember. And that's brand goodness, baked right in! (Sorry, couldn't help myself!)

Then comes **color palette**. Bright, sugary pinks and turquoise might scream "trendy cupcake shop," but your bakery is about heritage and comfort. It is anchored in a strong community. A warm palette of cream, gold, and deep brown communicates tradition, trust, and timelessness. That choice connects instantly with locals looking for a place that feels like home…and tastes even better!

Typography follows. Remember fonts matter more than most people realize. A bold, blocky sans-serif would feel cold and industrial here. Instead, a friendly serif typeface for headlines and a clean sans-serif for body copy strike an even balance: approachable yet professional. It says, "We've been around, and we're here for you tomorrow and beyond, too."

Next up? **Imagery Style**. Now, how do you present your story? Not with stock photos of baguettes from a library in Paris. Think local. Instead, your imagery shows your bakers kneading dough, your storefront on Main Street, and your customers breaking bread at Saturday morning tables. Real people, real place, real food. That authenticity makes the brand relatable.

Now, setting your sites on the brand's **Voice and Tone**. Your brand voice ties it all together. It's warm, neighborly, and lighthearted—like chatting with an old friend over coffee. Your social posts might highlight the day's specials with a touch of humor ("Come early, or Grandma Daisy will beat you to the pecan pie again!"). It's a tone that reinforces your position as part of the community, not just another storefront.

Finally, your **Design System** makes sure all of this stays consistent. From the color of your coffee cup sleeves to the typography in your flyers to the signage above the counter, everything aligns with the brand. Even if you let a local high school student design your seasonal cookie ad, they'll have a guide to ensure it matches the look, feel, and voice of your bakery. Your brand.

Individually, each element has its role. But together? They're a team. They form a cohesive identity that feels authentic, trustworthy, and memorable. When you commit to these seven elements, you stop relying on luck or random design choices. Instead, you give your brand a blueprint that resonates deeply with your community and sets you apart from the competition.

Conclusion

When you step back and look at the seven elements of brand identity, it's easy to see why they matter so much. They aren't just decorative pieces or "nice-to-haves." They are the **building blocks** of how your business shows up in the world—how your community recognizes you, remembers you, and ultimately decides whether or not to build a relationship with you.

For local businesses, this is even more vital. Unlike a national brand with a multi-million-dollar ad budget, you don't have the luxury of throwing mixed messages into the marketplace and hoping something sticks. Your brand identity must work harder, smarter, and more consistently, because every dollar and every impression counts.

Consider a local café who may feel as if it were time to "freshen things up." And let's face it: Brands do evolve. They need to. But they should always evolve with careful consideration to these seven brand elements. If this café introduces a trendy new logo, printed menus in six different fonts, paint the walls a color that clashes with their signage, and begin posting stock photos to social media...well, there could be more than coffee brewing. Too many off-brand changes so quickly can cause a problem. Why? Because none of it connected. That's not evolution; that's disruption. You see, with their fresh new look, their loyal regulars barely recognize the place. New customers? They walk away confused by the inconsistency. Within a year (probably less), the café runs the risk of needing another rebrand—not to "freshen things up" mind you, but to survive. Because by then, much of the trust they had built is gone.

The moral?

When you ignore consistency across these seven elements, you risk looking disorganized at best and untrustworthy at worst.

That's why these seven elements matter. Think of the Brand Elements as your storefront, even when people aren't standing in front of your physical door. Your logo, tagline, colors, fonts, and imagery are all signals to your audience. Your voice and design system are the glue that holds it together. Working in unison, they build familiarity. Familiarity builds trust. And trust builds loyalty. All speak to the heart of the relationship your brand is trying to build.

The truth is, people don't just buy products or services—they buy stories, experiences, and relationships. Your brand identity is the foundation of that story. When it's crafted with care and carried out with consistency, it creates a sense of belonging. It tells your community, **"This is who we are, this is what we stand for, and this is why you matter to us."**

So don't treat these seven elements as a checklist. Treat them as the DNA of your brand. They are what keep you from blending into the background and what give your business staying power in a crowded local marketplace.

As we move into the next chapter, we'll take the foundation you've built here and show you how to bring it to life through messaging. Because a strong identity doesn't just look good—it gives you the confidence to communicate clearly, consistently, and compellingly with your community.

4

Chapter 4: Clarifying Your Brand Message

A confused customer never buys. That's why message clarity is the cornerstone of brand success. Your brand message isn't just a catchy headline—it's a strategic narrative that communicates **who you are, what you do, and why it matters**—in a way that instantly clicks with your target audience.

Take an independent insurance carrier BrandVision Marketing worked with. There were several goals on the docket, chief among them increasing property and casualty clients as well as Life, Medicare and more. I love independent agents because they are not tied to a single entity. They're free to shop multiple carriers, compare rates, and act as a true advocate for their clients. It speaks to the heart of relationship, which is at the very core of a successful brand.

But the first thing I noticed? Messaging. Hmm…It was a steady stream of features and fear tactics: **"Protect against risk." "Avoid financial hardship." "Are you ready for untimely death?"**

Even the least skeptical consumers would think: "Yawn"… "Is it time to get up?"… "Well, not mine, but maybe this ad's!"

Consumers didn't feel a sense of connection—they felt
bored, or worse, tuned out. In other words, the messaging
failed to resonate with meaning and relevance. Why?
Because the message lacked the one ingredient that makes
people lean in: **emotion**.

In order to reach our goals for this client, it was all about
making the messaging culturally relevant to the consumer.
Now, I'm not talking about over-the-top emotive elements
that have you scared to peek out the front door. But I am
talking about emotional drivers that consumers relate easily
to—making them think more deeply about their situation
and how this agency might actually benefit them.

The fact is: people buy with emotion first and justify with
logic later. If your brand message doesn't speak to
something people care about—family, freedom, safety,
pride, convenience—it simply will not stick. That meant
shifting from sterile lines like "Protect against risk" to
relatable ones like: "Helping you make sure your
daughter's first car has protection that lets you sleep easy."

The difference is simple: One is insurance jargon. The
other is real life. And people live in real life.

That's the power of clarifying your brand message.

Why Clear Messaging Matters

- **Cuts through noise:** Clear messaging stands out in
  crowded markets.
- **Builds trust:** When people understand you quickly,
  they trust you faster.

- **Drives action:** People take action when they feel confident and understood.
- **Unifies teams:** A shared message ensures consistency across sales, marketing, and service. More on this later.

The Core Elements of a Clear Brand Message

The message truly matters and only a clear brand message is gold. Otherwise, confusion reigns. After all, your brand needs to stand for something in the minds of the consumers on Main Street; and what it stands for needs to **matter** to folks. Here are the five core elements that you should look to address in creating your Brand Message:

1. **The Problem You Solve**
   - Identify the Pain Points or challenges that your audience faces…that you solve.
   - Speak in their language—mirror the words they use to describe their struggles.
2. **The Solution You Offer**
   - Describe your product or service simply.
   - Don't rely on jargon; clarity beats cleverness.
3. **The Transformation**
   - Paint a picture of what success looks like after using your brand.
   - This is the emotional payoff—how their life or business improves.
4. **Proof and Credibility**
   - Show testimonials, stats, or credentials to support your claims.

- o The more genuine credibility you can demonstrate, the deeper the relationship with the brand will resonate with the consumer.
5. **Call to Action (CTA)**
   - o Be direct: What's the next step? Book a call? Try a demo? Visit your store? Make it easy to do business with you.

The Problem You Solve

The moment you flipped the sign to "Open for Business," you knew your job was to solve problems. Every customer who walks through your door—or clicks to your site— carries a Pain Point. Maybe it's a mild annoyance, maybe it's something that keeps them up at night. Either way, your brand exists to remove the obstacle and clear the path forward.

For the working parent, it might be an after-school program that keeps their 9-year-old son happy, engaged, and home before dinner instead of sulking about "that stupid daycare place."

For the accident victim, it could be seeking guidance, even protection, in facing down a fast-talking insurance company after last week's wreck—while nursing a sore back that's keeping them from coaching their daughter's softball team this season.

For the professional planning a big event, it's the pressure of finding a caterer who won't flop and tank their chances at a promotion.

Pain points are varied and many. Your job is to identify them and communicate—clearly—that you can solve them. That means mirroring the language your customers actually use. Speak like they speak. If they describe their frustration as "getting the runaround" or "never knowing what to expect," borrow those words in your messaging. Nothing creates connection faster than a customer feeling, "That's exactly what I've been thinking!"

For the parent, a daycare would highlight how kids at their program don't want to leave when pickup time comes. For the accident victim, a lawyer would emphasize that they protect the vulnerable and make sure the victim gets what they deserve—not what the insurance giant wants to hand out. For the event planner, a caterer would position themselves as the secret weapon that makes their client the office hero, with a spread that has everyone buzzing for weeks.

That's what clear messaging does—it doesn't dance around features. It speaks directly to the problem, shows empathy, and positions you as the solution. Because when your brand consistently solves problems in the eyes of your audience, you stop being "a business option" and start becoming the brand people can't imagine living without, which is exactly where you want to be.

The Solution You Offer

Once you've named the problem, you have to show how you fix it. Customers don't buy features; they buy outcomes. Your brand message should paint a clear picture of how life gets better once they choose you.

For the daycare parent, it's not about "our staff ratio is 1:12" or "we have certified employees." That's fine print. The solution is peace of mind—knowing their child is safe, happy, having fun, and maybe even learning something new before dinner.

For the accident victim, the solution isn't "we know personal injury law." It's the reassurance that someone will go toe-to-toe with the insurance company, so they can heal without financial stress.

For the event planner, the solution isn't "we have 25 years of catering experience." It's the confidence that their boss will rave about the menu instead of raise an eyebrow at the mistakes.

The key: speak to the outcome, not the ingredients. A common mistake is drowning in jargon or rattling off credentials. Those details matter later, but your brand message should spotlight transformation. The difference between **"we provide"** and **"you experience."**

Too many local businesses stop at saying what they do: "We mow lawns," "We sell insurance," "We bake donuts." That's not a solution—that's a category. Real solutions answer the deeper need: "We give you your weekends back," "We protect your family's future," "We make mornings taste better."

With that in mind, I'll put myself in the crosshairs for a bit.

"All I need to know is if the phone is ringing. Scott, you know marketing and advertising. That's why you're here. I know the law. You do what you do, so I don't have to deal with it. That way I can focus on doing what I do. So go do it. I don't need to know anything else."

That was a quote from one of my favorite clients of all time. I was going through our game plan for his personal injury law firm in incredible detail. But he didn't need a bunch of marketing jargon. He didn't care about CPP, CPM, Gross Impressions or any other marketing gobbledygook. He cared about one thing: He wanted the phone to ring—enough to secure 30 new clients a month. I'm proud to say, that was something that we were able to do for him time and time again.

But that exchange taught me something valuable about Messaging. Talk in terms the audience cares about and relates to. Everything else is very much unwanted noise.

Because when you show how positive life looks after you step in, you move from being a vendor to being a trusted partner.

The Transformation…Answering the "Why You" Question

Here's the tough part: customers are swimming in options. If you don't explain why you're different, you risk blending into the noidr. Your clear brand message has to answer the question every customer silently asks: **"Why should I choose you instead of the other guy?"**

It's all about results. Your customers want to see the other side of the story—what life looks like after you've solved their problem. Clear messaging paints that picture while creating discernment.

For the daycare, maybe it's a backyard garden where kids plant and eat their own vegetables—a learning experience no one else offers…all before group homework sessions and playtime. The parent takes notices and envisions a happy son and a calmer evening routine—homework already finished, dinner shared without stress, and a child who's excited to go back tomorrow.

For the attorney, maybe it's that you've settled more claims in the metro than anyone else. That's credibility **and** local proof. The accident victim thinks, 'peace of mind'…knowing their medical bills and car repairs are covered, and their family's finances are protected.

For the caterer, maybe it's your focus on farm-to-table ingredients from nearby growers, giving events a hometown flavor competitors can't copy. The event planner envisions an event leaving co-workers proudly saying, "This is the best company party we've ever had," all while the boss takes notice.

If you don't describe results, you leave the customer guessing. And when they guess, skepticism can reign. In other words, they usually assume less than you can actually deliver. Don't get me wrong—and word of warning: Over-promising is deadly to a brand. Do not create unrealistic expectations through fanciful promises. In no time, every ad will spark an instant eye-roll, accompanied by the ole 'yeah, right!' reaction…not at all where you want to be.

Instead: Deliver! Use your brand message to move people from "problem" to "promise." Show them not just what you do, but how their life will be better because of you. That is where connection happens. That doesn't generate the eye-roll; it spurs an elated eye-brow raise. (Much better!)

So, don't just offer a product or service—successful local branding is about positioning yourself as the answer.

Because when your audience believes you are the solution to their problem, they stop shopping and start choosing you.

Proof and Credibility

You've said you can solve the problem. You've explained how you're different. Now people want proof. Trust comes faster when you can back up your promises with evidence.

Proof can take many forms:

- ❖ **Testimonials from real customers**—*bonus points if they're recognizable locals…because piggy-backing on the words of those who already have trust within the community is a big win*
- ❖ **Before-and-after examples**—*showing transformation is strong*
- ❖ **Numbers and results**—*"we've helped 327 families find affordable coverage this year"*
- ❖ **Case studies or even simple stories**—*use tales that resonate with people because they can instantly put themselves in the main character's shoes*

For the daycare, that might be a parent saying, "Now, my son begs me to be late in picking him up—he loves it here."

For the attorney, it might be, "We've won $10 million in settlements for local clients."

For the caterer, maybe it's a photo gallery of glowing events and a quote from a well-known HR director: "You made me look like a superstar."

Without proof, your message risks feeling like fluff. With proof, it becomes believable. And in local markets, word-of-mouth proof is golden. Your reputation becomes your marketing.

The danger? Claiming "great service" or "quality you can trust." Everyone says that. It's not distinctive, it's wallpaper. Instead, find the distinguishable angle that only you can claim—and tie it back to the customer's world.

Because difference isn't about being louder—it's about being more distinctive and more relevant.

A Clear Call to Action

Even the best message fails if people don't know what to do next. Your brand message must always point to a clear next step that is easily taken.

For the daycare: "Schedule a free after-school visit—let your child test-drive the fun."

For the attorney: "Call today for a free consultation—don't let the insurance company push you around."

For the caterer: "Book your tasting this week and cross one big stressor off your event checklist."

Too often, local businesses get shy here. They bury **the ask** in polite phrasing like "feel free to reach out" or "we'd love to talk." The problem? Ambiguity doesn't move people.

You don't need to be pushy. That's a turn-off, but a clear, direct **call to action** does move the needle toward action.

Tell them exactly what to do, and make it easy. A confused customer never buys—but a confident one takes the next step.

Wrap Up

When you tie these five elements together—Problem, Solution, Transformation, Proof, and Call to Action—you've got the foundation of a clear, powerful brand message. Skip one, and you risk leaving customers guessing. Nail all five, and you give people the clarity they crave and the confidence to choose you.

Conclusion

When you boil it down, clear brand messaging isn't about being clever—it's about being understood. Clarity rules the day. Each of the five elements plays its part in making that happen:

- ✓ **The Problem You Solve...** This shows your audience that you "get it." You understand their Paint Point...their struggles, frustrations, or aspirations.
- ✓ **The Solution You Offer...** Now, you step in to ease that Pain Point—the reason your business exists in the first place.

✓ **The Transformation...** Next, you make the value personal, shifting focus from what you do to what your customers gain.
✓ **Proof and Credibility...** It's time to prove your case...all while keeping you from sounding like every other "me too" competitor down the street. It gives people a reason to choose **you**.
✓ **Call to Action (CTA)...**Finally, remove guesswork and make it easy for someone to take the next step instead of drifting away.

Individually, these elements are useful. Together, they're powerful. They form a narrative that guides your customer from problem to solution, from doubt to trust, from "maybe" to "yes."

Think of your message as a conversation with the people you want to reach. If you talk only about yourself, they tune out. But when you clarify the problem, position your solution, highlight benefits, show your unique strengths, and give them a clear next step—you're no longer selling, you're guiding. And people love to follow a clear, confident guide.

That's the heart of brand messaging: taking out that machete and clearing a distinct path for your customer to follow...essentially building a bridge between what you offer and what your customers truly need. When your message is clear, it cuts through the noise, builds trust, and moves people to action.

Find an easy to reference checklist to help you guide your messaging at **Appendix A** on page 180.

Next, in Chapter 5, we'll flip the coin and look at what **not** to do—the common messaging blunders that can derail even the best-intentioned brand. Spotting these mistakes early will save you time, money, and a lot of frustration.

5

Chapter 5: Avoiding Common Messaging Blunders

When we begin working with a new client, one of the first things we do is assess their current program. Sure, sometimes BrandVision Marketing is brought in to wear the marketing hat because the client is already wearing four other hats atop one noggin. But quite often, we're brought in because there is an issue that has stymied revenue and results.

There are several factors we look for. Sometimes it's a lack of continuity. Often it's a lack of focus. At times, though it is the brand messaging.

Even the best intentions can get lost in translation if your brand message misses the mark. Local businesses don't usually fail because they don't care, but because their messaging gets cluttered, confusing, or simply disconnects from what their audience actually needs. Flying around the Pain Point without ever landing does nothing to drive the consumer…or sales. However, good messaging can.

Yes, good messaging delivers because it connects. It resonates. It speaks directly to a consumer's Pain Point and says very clearly, "We can help you with that…and here is how!"

That is what good, clear messaging is supposed to do— deliver a specific solution…(YOU!), to a specific consumer problem. Following the 5 elements for clarifying your brand message will set you on the right path, for certain. Avoiding the messaging stumbling blocks will, too.

Below are some of the most common traps I've seen businesses fall into. Think of these as potholes on the brand highway—if you know where they are, you can steer around them and keep your messaging strategy on course.

😠 Speaking in Features Instead of Benefits

It's tempting to rattle off what you do: "We offer 24/7 service, licensed technicians, and free estimates." Great—but so does everyone else. Customers aren't lying awake at night wishing for "licensed technicians." That's great, of course, but honestly, it's expected. It doesn't move the needle. Worry does. And what they worry about is a burst pipe flooding their basement.

The feature tells what you do. The benefit tells what it means to the customer. **Focus on the latter**.

☞ Example: Instead of saying "24/7 Service," say, "When your furnace quits at 2 a.m., we'll be there before your coffee pot finishes brewing."

🔊 *True Story*... We worked with a local women's fitness center whose marketing leaned heavily on features—lists of hours, equipment, and class schedules. Those things matter, but they're not what grabs attention. Features are verifiers, not motivators. They belong **after** you've sparked interest.

When we shifted the messaging to focus on emotional drivers—"feeling stronger," "boosting confidence," "building better health"—the connection clicked. Those phrases spoke to what women in the community actually wanted, not just when the gym doors were open. The features still played their role on the back end, but the emotional hook did the heavy lifting.

The result? A 24% increase in enrollment in just two months. Proof that when you lead with benefits and feelings, features naturally fall into place.

😑 Using Buzzwords and Jargon

If your customer needs a dictionary to understand you, you've already lost them. Buzzwords like "synergy," "hit the ground," or "easy-to-use" might sound impressive in the boardroom, but on Main Street they fall flat. Worse, jargon can create a wall between you and your audience, making you look aloof or out of touch.

☞ Example: A chiropractor that says "We specialize in holistic integrative neuromusculoskeletal realignment" is bound to get blank stares. But "We help people get rid of back pain and feel like themselves again" is instantly relatable.

🔊 *True Story*... The IT world is full of brilliant minds— and big egos. Too often, that shows up in marketing that sounds like a jargon-filled lecture designed more to impress peers than connect with customers. That's fine for Freud's battle of the ego, super ego, and id, but small business owners don't have time to decode cryptic tech speak.

When we partnered with a local IT provider, the challenge wasn't to "dumb things down," but to simplify and clarify. We focused on what their services actually **meant** for business owners: less downtime, more security, and peace of mind. The shift made clients feel empowered not confused.

The outcome? Prospects stopped tuning out, and the provider gained traction with an audience that finally understood the real value of partnering with them.

😑 Trying to Be All Things to All People

You can't be the cheapest, the fastest, the most luxurious, and the most reliable all at once. Yet many businesses scatter their message so broadly that no single point comes across clearly. This creates confusion—and remember, a confused customer never buys.

☞ Example: A restaurant that markets itself as "fine dining, casual family-friendly, and fast takeout" leaves people wondering, **what is it really?** Focus on one lane, own it, and build your reputation there.

🔊 *True Story*... When BrandVision Marketing began working with a local realtor, their messaging was scattered. They wanted to appeal to everyone—from first-time buyers to luxury estate clients—but in trying to speak to all audiences at once, they spoke clearly to none. The result? Confused messaging that blended into the noise.

Our solution was to build a clear brand "umbrella." His personal brand—trustworthy, approachable, relationship-driven—became the anchor. Under that umbrella, we created tailored messaging for each segment: simple, reassuring brochures for first-time buyers, prestige-driven pieces for high-end clients, and family-focused campaigns for move-up buyers.

By clarifying the overarching brand while tailoring the message where it mattered, the realtor was able to position himself as both focused and versatile. He stopped being just another face on a yard sign and became the go-to solution across segments with one brand voice.

☹ Copying Competitors

It's natural to keep an eye on the other guy. But too often, businesses mimic the competition so closely that they lose their own identity. When your logo, tagline, or website reads like a carbon copy of the shop down the street, you become forgettable. Differentiation is the lifeblood of branding—without it, you're just another option in a crowded market.

☞ Example: If three realtors in your town use the tagline "Your Hometown Realtor," then a fourth adding the same line isn't branding—it's blending. A stronger approach would highlight what makes **you** distinct: "Helping families find their forever home since 1998."

🔊 *True Story*...The personal injury law category is a challenging one for many, many reasons. One reason? Well, it's a category without many distinctive brands and thus susceptible to competitors simply buying market share with exorbitant ad budgets.

One of our clients faced this very challenge when a local competitor began running shock-value ads, making outrageous claims. Now, we had established a solid brand footing in the market, so we didn't see a dip in new cases walking through the door. However, the firm was certainly concerned and even floated the idea of creating similar messaging...or at least calling out the other guy's extreme ads.

That would have been a big mistake and I'm glad we didn't head in that direction. Yes, the competition did create buzz with their outrageousness, but we kept our message consistent and on-brand—the same brand that had already garnered a strong market reputation. (And calling out the competition? Even if you're disparaging them, it's just throwing dollars their way. It's like saying, "Don't think about pink elephants!" Now, what did you just think of? The Defense rests.)

😑 Inconsistent Messaging Across Channels

Your website says one thing, your ads say another, and your staff says something completely different. That inconsistency erodes trust. Customers should hear and feel the same brand voice whether they're scrolling your

Facebook page, talking to an employee, or opening a direct mail piece.

☞ Example: Imagine a fitness center that promotes itself online as a friendly, judgment-free zone—only to have staff members raising those eyebrows of cynicism while using intimidating, hardcore language in person. That disconnect undermines the brand promise.

◀⁾⁾ *True Story*...One of the strategies BrandVision Marketing uses to evaluate whether a brand is truly being **lived** is Mystery Shopping. We send individuals into a client's business with a specific scenario—a situation the staff should be able to handle within the parameters of the brand promise.

The feedback we get is always helpful, whether it's reinforcing or we need to tweak the customer service approach. Once, while evaluating a community bank, we witnessed the latter from several branches. The bank's positioning was centered on "going the extra mile"—a warm, helpful focus. But here's what one shopper heard when asking about an auto loan: "You might want to check with a credit union. They usually have better rates."

Ouch. That's not just off-message—that's pushing business to the competition.

Now, to be fair, the issues we uncovered were easily fixable with training and clearer internal alignment. But the lesson is powerful: when your messaging isn't consistent with the actual customer experience, you're wasting valuable marketing dollars.

If you promise family-style service, but your employees act dismissive, the brand collapses under the weight of its own inconsistency. If your ads say one thing while your website and frontline staff say another, you're confusing customers and eroding trust.

Continuity matters. From your brochure and social media to streaming ads, billboards, and face-to-face interactions, the brand must feel the same across every touchpoint. That's how you turn a message into a reputation—and a reputation into a relationship that builds a powerful brand.

😣 Forgetting the Emotional Hook

In the marketing fantasy realm, we would all like to think that consumer's make very logical, rational decisions with their money. Further, we like to think that those brands that make a rational case to the consumer will, indeed, easily earn their business and those valuable dollars.

Spoiler alert: **That does not happen!**

So, making **logic** your 'go-to' brand messaging strategy? Well, logic makes people think, but emotion makes people act. Too many businesses settle for transactional messaging: "We sell tires," "We offer accounting services," or "We build websites." Yes, but **why does it matter?** Instead, explore the deeper benefit and bring that emotional tie into clear focus. Safe travels with your family. Peace of mind at tax time. A digital storefront that gets you noticed.

Emotional clarity is what moves a customer from "maybe" to "yes."

☞ Example: Instead of "Affordable tires," try "Drive your kids to school every morning with confidence." One speaks to the wallet, the other to the heart.

🔊 *True Story*...I am a big fan of testimonial ads. Regardless of category or place on the brand spectrum— whether the client is a start-up brand or one closing in on Cash Cow status, I love hearing customers glow to other, prospective customers about their own fandom of a brand.

It is a simple fact of life: When you talk about how great you are, it is not nearly as impressive as other people talking about your greatness. The first lands as flat and implausible, if not finger-nails on chalkboard cringe worthy. The latter? It resonates.

When we use testimonials as a messaging strategy, we always try to address typical objections that a company may experience. Inevitably, **speaking to specific and common concerns** by an unpaid spokesperson about their experiences is gold. "I only wish I would have called sooner and saved myself so much worry" That speaks to the heart of their experience and may push some procrastinators across the finish line.

That's what emotion can and should do for your messaging.

The Bottom Line

Clear, consistent, emotionally relevant messaging is the difference between being ignored and being remembered. Avoid the traps of feature-heavy copy, buzzwords, copycatting, and inconsistency. Instead, speak your customer's language through your unique brand voice. Highlight the problems you solve, and deliver your message with clarity across every touchpoint.

When you do, you give your brand the power to cut through the noise and claim its own space in the mind of your community. And that means the coveted manila folder in the consumer's mind thickens in a resoundingly positive way.

Getting Everyone on the Same Page

At BrandVision Marketing, we've built our process around three stages for creating, shifting, or refreshing a brand. The first, as you've seen, is **BrandFOCUS**—the research phase that gives us a profitable direction. The second is **BrandTRAINING**—where we take that direction and teach the people who will bring it to life how to actually **live the brand**. Who are those people? Your employees, of course.

Why does this matter? Because the expectations created by messaging must match the experiences. You can't claim to be a "family-friendly" brand if every other customer who walks through the door gets the black-sheep treatment. Sure, that may feel authentic to certain families (we've all been there), but as a branding strategy? Not productive!

That's why we create a **Brand Guideline Book** (see page 89) for our clients and then train employees on what the brand stands for, what its voice sounds like, and how it should show up in different situations.

The fact is: employees are the most important brand ambassadors you have. More important than ads. More vital than color schemes and logos. Everything uncovered in the research phase is wasted if the people who interact with your customers ignore it, dismiss it, or—worst of all— contradict it.

Think back to that "manila folder of the mind." Each customer interaction adds another page. If those interactions are inconsistent, the folder becomes jumbled. But when employees embody the brand voice and values, every page tells the same story—and the relationship grows stronger.

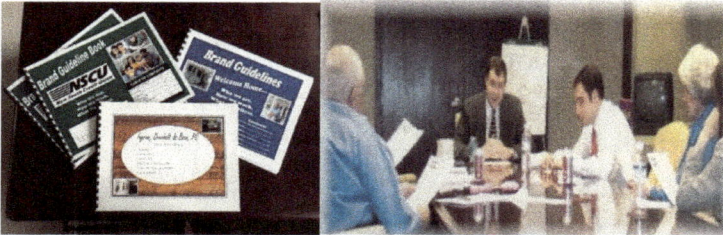

Every interaction—even the tough ones—present an opportunity. Done right, even conflict can **strengthen** the brand because customers see consistency under pressure.

That's the power of **Brand****TRAINING**: aligning employees with the brand voice, giving them clear expectations, and equipping them to live the brand every day at every turn. So, train your staff on living the brand. Most employees truly want to be positive brand ambassadors for you. They do. Training gives them a compass to do exactly that.

◀)) *True Story*...A local accounting firm hired BrandVision Marketing to conduct **Brand**TRAINING. Their identity was clear on paper—professional, trustworthy, dependable—and they wanted to avoid a customer experience that felt like the stereotypical "boring accountant" routine. They wanted to accentuate their relationship-centric approach with clients and end comparisons equating an accounting firm with stepping into a library...quiet, efficient, but not exactly warm or inviting.

Through **Brand**TRAINING, we helped their team embrace a lighter, more approachable side of the brand. We showed them how small touches of humor, everyday friendliness, and conversational language could bring their "Trusted Advisor" identity to life, doing so in a fun way—essentially adopting a mindset of "Taking what you do seriously without taking yourself too seriously."

We used interactive exercises in training sessions and role-played everything from greeting clients with warmth to breaking down complex tax topics in plain, nonsensical English. Employees got into it—one even joked, "I never thought I'd be practicing stand-up comedy at an accounting workshop!"

The results? Immediate. Clients began commenting that the firm felt more personable, less intimidating, and easier to work with. Satisfaction scores climbed, and referrals increased because people weren't just impressed with the firm's expertise—they enjoyed the experience.

The lesson? Even in industries known for seriousness, living your brand can mean finding a balance between professionalism and personality. When employees lean into that balance, the brand shines brighter than ever before.

Quick Wins: Creating Conversations that Connect & Convert

Focusing on the five elements of clear brand messaging—while steering clear of the six pitfalls we discussed—is a formula for a strong communication foundation. Once your message is crystal clear, you're ready to put it into action—building campaigns, ads, and conversations that not only connect but also convert. Here are some practical "wins" you can put into play immediately:

Crafting a Simple Brand Script

Keep it simple. Use this plug-and-play formula as a foundation:

"We help [target audience] solve [problem] by providing [solution], so they can achieve [desired outcome]."

Example: "We help busy parents find flexible after-school care by providing fun, safe, and enriching programs, so they can work without guilt and know their kids are happy."

☞ **Pro tip** Post your script above your desk. If a message doesn't align with it, rewrite until it does.

Storytelling Frameworks That Work

Your brand isn't the hero—your **customer** is. One of the most effective messaging tools is the *StoryBrand Framework* by Donald Miller. It casts your customer as the hero and your brand as merely the guide. The structure is:

1. A Character (the customer)
2. Has a Problem
3. Meets a Guide (your brand)
4. Who Gives Them a Plan
5. And Calls Them to Action
6. That Ends in Success
7. Or Helps Them Avoid Failure

This narrative approach helps your audience see themselves in your messaging and imagine success with your help.

A local roofing company, for example, could say: "Your home is your castle—but a leaky roof makes it vulnerable. We inspect, repair, and replace with care, so your family stays safe and dry no matter the storm." It's a story every homeowner can see themselves in.

Brand Message vs. Tagline vs. Elevator Pitch

Each plays a unique role, but all must hum the same tune:

Brand Message: The full "why we exist" and "what we deliver."

Tagline: A short, punchy, and sticky line that sets you apart from the competition. ("Fresh. Fast. Friendly.")

Elevator Pitch: A 20–30 second spoken version you can deliver over coffee or at a Chamber mixer.

Once upon a time, I did a lot of networking, participating in a lot of business-building groups. My Elevator Pitch in those settings? Here it is: "BrandVision Marketing is a full-service agency that serves as an extension of our client's marketing department. We work with small-to-mid sized businesses whose owners are wearing many hats—they simply do not have time to wear that marketing hat as well. So, they make one call and we do the heavy lifting. They focus on their business—while we handle everything from their business cards to multi-media ad campaigns…all with a brand-focus in mind. Anything a marketing department would handle—BrandVision Marketing manages."

☞ **Pro tip:** Test your elevator pitch on a stranger. If they can repeat it back in their own words, you've nailed it.

Clear Calls-to-Action (CTAs)

Don't leave people hanging. Tell them **exactly** what you want them to do next. Whether it's "Call Today," "Book Your Free Estimate," or "Join Our Weekly Email," a clear CTA makes the path forward obvious.

Bad CTA: "Learn more."

Better CTA: "Schedule your free 15-minute consultation today."

Avoid These Messaging Missteps

- Talking too much about **yourself** instead of your customer's Pain Points.
- Overloading your message with industry jargon.
- Trying to cram five points into one sentence.
- Forgetting a CTA.

Examples of Clear Messaging

- **Slack**: "Slack brings the team together, wherever you are."
- **Airbnb**: "Belong anywhere."
- **Evernote**: "Remember everything."
- **Local Example**: Coffee shop: "Helping Lexington wake up one cup at a time."
- **Local Example**: Boutique gym: "A stronger, healthier, and happier YOU—right here at home."

Conclusion

Clear messaging helps people instantly understand what you do and why it matters. It's not about being the loudest—it's about being the clearest. If a stranger can't "get it" in five seconds, you've still got work to do. When you get it right, you'll notice the shift—conversations start flowing more easily, referrals come quicker, and customers engage more deeply.

Check out Appendix A on page 180 for a quick reference checklist to ensure you are avoiding the six pitfalls.

In the next chapter, we'll look at the psychology behind **why** branding works—and how to harness it to your advantage.

6

Chapter 6: The Psychology of Branding

People don't buy products. They buy what those products mean. But the sheer psychology of branding comes with its fair share of blind spots. And trust me, brands do, indeed, have blind spots.

Case in point: Once I broke out a brand new razor before my Sunday morning shave before heading to church. I gave myself one last look in the rearview mirror, saw one fine-looking dude (yes, roll your eyes—even I couldn't write that with a straight face), and strutted inside like all was well. There, I was my normal social butterfly self, chatting it up as usual. Sure, a few folks seemed a little standoffish, but I chalked that up to them "having a bad day" and went about my way. That 'way' took me to Taco Bell for a quick lunch pick-up.

Usually, I would go out to eat with friends after church, but no one asked and I pivoted, right? No biggie. I placed my order and pulled up to the drive-thru window. As the little teen girl reached for my money, she exclaimed, "**OH MY GOSH**! What happened to **YOU**!" To which I quickly got a full look at my face in the visor mirror, suddenly realizing that I was completely bloody from the nose down! That new razor had butchered my entire face and neck.

The church crowd didn't say a word—whether out of kindness, awkwardness, or just not noticing. Although, I assure you, it was not the latter! But the teenager? Zero filter. Brands face this too: your loyal audience might overlook flaws out of goodwill and built-in equity, but new or less invested prospects will call them out without hesitation. Or worse—ignore your brand completely. So, your brand's psychology needs to account for all audiences: from the forgiving fans to the blunt newcomers to those omni-present ghosts.

Step one? You have to ask yourself: What does your brand mean, psychologically?

After all, a cup of coffee isn't just caffeine in a paper cup— it's your wakeup call…it's warmth on a cold morning, or five stolen minutes of peace amid chaos. If you're wearing Nike's, you're wearing everything that brand stands for— not just a pair of shoes made of leather and rubber. No, that brand is about confidence, status, or the freedom to run farther than ever before. And your local brand? It carries its own unique meaning too. The real work is uncovering it, shaping it, and making sure every audience sees it clearly.

Whenever I conduct a **Brand**Training session, I ask employees to pause and consider the difference between the **function** of their job and the **meaning** behind it. A bank teller may think she's just depositing a paycheck. A paralegal may feel like he's simply jotting down details from an accident report. An insurance agent may assume she's only selling a policy to a pair of newlyweds. But there's always more at play.

That "more" is the shift from transaction to transformation. When the teller realizes she's providing peace of mind for the customer (that the bills will be paid)…when the paralegal sees himself as the first reassuring voice to calm a shaken client…when the insurance agent recognizes she's helping a couple step into their new life with security and hope—that's when ordinary interactions become meaningful moments. And that's when brands step up—because they stop being logos and start becoming relationships.

This shift is psychological. After all, why do people choose one brand over another when the products or services are nearly identical? The answer lies in **psychology**. It rests on how those brands make people **feel**. Whether on the local or national level, great branding isn't just about how your business looks or sounds—it's about how it **connects** with the deeper needs and desires of the human mind.

Understanding the psychological drivers behind brand perception can transform how you build and communicate your brand.

Why Psychology Matters in Branding

Branding is about influencing perception; and doing so in a very truistic way…if you want the brand to thrive, that is. Every color, word, and image you use triggers subconscious associations and emotions. And through it all runs one constant: relationship. Brands are relationships—but a unique kind. Think of it like that cutie in homeroom back in your school days. You only get a few chances to make an impression, and whether or not they're open to connecting, you've got to try, right?

Now, you could show up in a neon green banana costume. Sure, you'll get noticed—but probably not for the reasons you want. The goal isn't shock value. It's building rapport in a way that sparks real connection, not temporary curiosity.

That's what branding does. It's about nudging, poking, and prodding—strategically—so that your brand gets noticed for the right reasons…and the relationship begins to form. Done well, branding moves past surface attention and into building a meaningful connection.

Here's how psychology plays its part. Smart branding taps into four key principles to:

- **Build emotional connections** – Because people don't just buy products, they buy feelings. The right emotional hook makes your brand unforgettable.
- **Create memorability** – First impressions are vital, but they can fade fast; memorability ensures your brand sticks long after the ad disappears.
- **Drive decision-making** – Small cues can tip the scales. Understanding how customers actually decide helps you guide them toward "yes."
- **Increase loyalty** – True loyalty isn't about discounts; it's about trust, identity, and belonging.

Emotions > Logic

In today's noisy world, logic rarely wins the day. Emotions guide behavior—and psychology helps you harness them.

When it comes to decision-making, we humans like to think we're rational creatures. Truth is, most of us are emotional first and logical second. We **buy** with our hearts and then **justify** with our heads. That shirt? You didn't throw down your credit card because it was versatile enough to go with multiple outfits. No. You bought it because it made you feel confident. That car? It wasn't just about horsepower; it was about the pride you'd feel pulling into the driveway.

The same is true for your customers. They may believe they're comparing features and crunching numbers—but under the surface, emotions call the shots. Don't get me wrong. Logic quickly swoops in soon afterward to validate the choice, leaving you often believing your decision was more than rational and certainly soundly justified.

Accepting this truth is step one toward effective brand communication. Step two? Finding the right emotional hook to make your brand distinctive and relevant. When you align your brand with an emotional driver that resonates with your audience's Pain Points, you stop shouting random messages at people and start connecting with them.

But here's the catch: emotions are powerful, and power must be handled wisely. Push too hard on fear or guilt, and you risk coming off as manipulative. Not a great way to build a relationship, right? Strike the right balance, and you position your brand as the guide who helps customers reach a more satisfied emotional place—a state of well-being that not only makes loyalty possible, but a **sure thing**.

So, what emotional battles are your prospects fighting? An insurance agent's customers might be craving **security and peace of mind**. A clothing manufacturer's customers might want **status, confidence, or a sense of belonging**. Every industry has its own emotional triggers.

Below is a quick-reference guide—a cheat sheet of 20+ industries and the emotional levers that typically drive consumer decisions.

CORE EMOTIONAL DRIVERS:

1. **Insurance** – security, peace of mind, protection
2. **Banking/Financial Services** – trust, strength, stability, empowerment, future confidence
3. **Healthcare/Medical Practices** – safety, relief, hope, compassion
4. **Restaurants/Dining** – comfort, indulgence, togetherness, adventure
5. **Fitness/Gyms** – confidence, vitality, self-improvement, belonging
6. **Automotive Sales/Repair** – freedom, reliability, pride, safety
7. **Real Estate** – security, aspiration, achievement, belonging, ascendency
8. **Travel/Tourism** – escape, joy, discovery, status, adventure, experience
9. **Hospitality/Hotels** – comfort, pampering, relaxation, prestige
10. **Clothing/Fashion** – confidence, individuality, attraction, fitting in/out
11. **Jewelry/Luxury Goods** – prestige, love, celebration, uniqueness
12. **Technology/IT Services** – empowerment, simplicity, relief, control
13. **Education/Tutoring** – hope, growth, achievement, pride
14. **Childcare/Daycare** – trust, safety, relief, joy
15. **Senior Care/Assisted Living** – dignity, security, compassion, family

16. **Home Improvement/Contractors** – pride, safety, control, comfort
17. **Landscaping/Gardening** – pride, peace, joy, harmony
18. **Restaurants/Bakeries** – nostalgia, indulgence, comfort, community
19. **Entertainment (Movies/Events)** – excitement, escape, joy, belonging
20. **Sports Teams/Leagues** – pride, unity, belonging, thrill, competitiveness
21. **Nonprofits/Charities** – compassion, purpose, impact, hope
22. **Legal Services** – protection, advocacy, fairness, empowerment
23. **Automotive Dealerships** – pride, freedom, achievement, safety
24. **Retail Stores (Local Shops)** – discovery, community, trust, value
25. **Beauty/Personal Care** – confidence, attraction, renewal, self-love

Create Memorability

First impressions matter…big time. But they can fade fast in the cluttered world of product and service offerings available for today's consumer. Memorability must be a goal. It ensures your brand lingers in the mind long after the ad disappears. After all, you want the consumer to neatly and distinctly label that manila folder of the mind, right? No one wants to get lost in a pile of files labeled 'generic'. No. That folder absolutely has to have your brand boldly written on the tab.

Memorability is that bold marker on the tab.

Connecting with your prospects memorably means connecting with them in a meaningful way. Memorability doesn't always mean being the loudest voice in the room. It does mean being the most meaningful. It's about connecting with your audience in a way that resonates—addressing Pain Points they actually care about, sparking those "Aha!" moments when the problem arises and your brand comes to mind as the answer.

Yes, you can be loud, funny, or entertaining—and those can work! And honestly, that may be a good long-term strategy that drives memorability. But keep in mind, 'funny' and 'entertaining' requires constant updating to keep the laughs rolling or else you get quickly tuned out. And that is not the goal. (Take it from a little boy who was a big joke teller! I always wanted to make people laugh. Still do. As a cute five-year-old, I could get away with a lot, but telling the same joke over and over? Even I was told to come up with some new material!) So, address Pain Points and focus on building the relationship...the brand...by being a helpful resource that has those answers.

The real path to memorability is linking your brand to consistent, helpful, relevant associations. For local brands, this can be as simple as:

- A landscaping company whose green trucks and sunflower logo become more than a familiar sight around town, but a staple.
- A bakery known for giving away donut holes to kids every Saturday morning.
- A realtor who always leaves a signature promotional product like a nice cutting board as a "welcome home" gift after closing.

- A local clothing retailer that serves tea, lattes and healthy snacks in its dressing room.
- The community bank that hosts the local school choir to sing Christmas Songs to their patrons during the holiday season.
- A local law firm that conducts a fundraising drive every year to benefit a local charity.

These aren't just tactics; they're memory triggers—small, repeatable moments that help your brand become part of the community's story.

The flip side? Well, brands that fail to be memorable fade fast. If your messaging is full of jargon...if your visuals look like everyone else's, or your customer experience is hit-or-miss? Then, you'll blend into the background. And in branding, being forgettable can be worse than being disliked.

So ask yourself: *What's the one thing I want people to remember when they walk away from my business?* That is your starting point for building a brand that sticks.

Memorability Checklist

Use this quick list to gauge whether your brand is leaving a lasting impression:

- ✓ **Distinct visuals:** Do your logo, colors, and typography stand out—or blend in with competitors?
- ✓ **Signature touchpoint:** Is there a unique, repeatable detail (like packaging, greetings, or giveaways) that people will associate only with your brand?

✓ **Emotional connection:** Does your messaging tap into feelings (security, joy, pride, relief) rather than just facts?

✓ **Consistency:** Are you delivering the same look, feel, and message across every touchpoint—ads, social, in-store, and customer service? Remember, continuity matters within every interaction.

✓ **Story-driven content:** Do you share stories that make your brand relatable and easy to remember?

✓ **Simplicity:** Can customers describe what you do and why it matters in one clear sentence?

✓ **Community presence:** Do people in your local market **see** and **experience** your brand regularly, in ways that feel authentic?

☞ If you can't check at least 5 of these memorability triggers with confidence, it's time to refine and sharpen your brand strategy.

Drive decision-making

Humans are vastly different creatures. This is true in many ways, but especially whereas decision-making is concerned. There is, however, a framework that we can examine, using those cues to tip the scale toward the sale. After all, if you understand how customers actually decide on the product or service in your category, you have a jump on guiding them toward a "yes."

There are essentially five steps every consumer will engage with when it's time to make a decision. Here they are:

STEP 1…What's Your Problem? The consumer recognizes a problem, a need, or a Pain Point that prompts them to begin a quest for a solution and subsequently being open to opening their wallet. This awareness can certainly arise from a direct, personal need, but can also be based on external stimuli (such as seeing an advertisement that sparks a desire).

STEP 2...*Find a Possible Solution!* Once the consumer realizes that trouble is afoot, it's time to seek potential solutions. This means gathering information from a variety of sources, including their own network or connections, as well as, internet searches, marketing materials and even online reviews. During this step, the consumer may rely on both internal and external resources to spark a game plan, leading them to...

STEP 3...*What are My Options?* Now, it's time for the consumer to compare different offerings within the category. What are my criteria for selection? Price? Quality? Features? Benefits? Which one(s) best meets their needs? What are the advantages and disadvantages of each option? With this data in tow, the consumer is able to narrow their options.

STEP 4...*Eureka! I've Found It!* After evaluating the different alternatives, the consumer makes the final decision. They've examined everything from Widget A to Widget Z and proceed with the purchase. It should be noted that this decision can be influenced by various factors. These include peer influence, marketing efforts, brand value, perceived value and more. It's important to know these factors for your category because addressing them through your marketing efforts can become critical.

STEP 5...*What Have I Done?!?* Finally, it's time to evaluate the purchase. Does the consumer love it? Hate it? Regret not going with the more expensive option? Regret spending too much money on this selection? All are bantered around the consumer's noggin as they reflect on their experience with the product or service. They assess their satisfaction level, which is a strong influencer on future purchasing decisions and brand loyalty—making post-sale contact important for most brands as positive experiences may lead to repeat purchases, while negative experiences? Well, those lead to returns and/or negative word-of-mouth.

Increase Loyalty

You've welcomed the consumer into your brand's fold. Now comes the bigger challenge: keeping them there.

Loyalty programs are everywhere today, but true loyalty isn't bought with points or discounts. Those create transactional loyalty, where customers stick around only as long as the deal is better than the other guy's. Real brand allegiance comes from emotional loyalty—a mix of trust, identity, and belonging.

Think about it. People don't wear a Nike swoosh because they saved 20%. They wear it because it makes them feel like an athlete, a doer, a winner. That's the kind of emotional resonance you want to build, even at the local level.

How? By creating connection points that go beyond the transaction. Ideally, your brand should foster a sense of community—customers who come back not just to buy from you, but to identify with you. Social media makes this easier than ever. Whether it's a bakery showcasing customer photos, a boutique spotlighting regulars, or a fitness center celebrating member milestones, brands that invite their audience into the story build bonds that outlast any coupon.

Now, not every industry lends itself to Instagram-worthy moments. Let's be real: legal, banking, and insurance fall more into the "have-to" category than the "want-to" category. You don't usually see someone say, "I can't wait to hang out at my credit union on Saturday!" And yet, loyalty in these spaces may be even more valuable— because when customers trust you in critical moments, they stick for life.

So, what can local businesses do to nurture that trust and belonging? A few simple, practical steps:

- ✓ **Consistency matters.** Every touchpoint, from your receptionist's greeting to your email newsletters, should feel "on brand." Customers should never wonder which version of you they're getting.
- ✓ **Show up when it counts.** Loyalty is often cemented in times of stress. That's why a community bank officer who answers their cell phone on a Saturday, or a lawyer who takes five extra minutes to explain the process, wins lifelong advocates.
- ✓ **Create micro-rituals.** Something as simple as a handwritten thank-you card, a birthday email, or remembering a client's favorite order can become part of your loyalty DNA.

When you approach loyalty as something to earn rather than something to buy, you stop worrying about competitors with deeper pockets poaching your customers. Discounts fade, but trust and belonging endure.

Key Psychological Factors Driving Your Brand's Creative Campaign

Every campaign comes to life with the creation of the actual marketing—the ads, the social media posts, the website and more. Applying the preceding 4 Principles is the oxygen that breathes life into your campaign. That, my friends, is challenging. Here are seven ways to do so…hit on as many of these as you can to build a campaign that rings your brand message loudly, clearly and with great connection:

1. **The Halo Effect**
   When people have a positive impression of one aspect of your brand (like memorable packaging or a helpful customer service experience), they often project that into the rest of the brand. They tend to assume that the rest of your brand is positive too. This is why consistent design and messaging matter—first impressions spill over and that's big. After all, you're not always going to hit a home run. But if you can effectively use the Halo Effect, mediocre aspects of your brand will begin looking like big winners by association.
2. **Cognitive Fluency**
   Brands that are easy to understand and recognize feel more trustworthy. Why? Well, because they are. Let's face it: when considering your own

personal relationships, if you greet a friend one morning and receive a big hug, then greet him the next morning and get a big slap in the face, you're left with confusion, right? It's same in the branding world. When consistent brand messaging, voice and personality rule the day, trust builds. Confusing messaging? Inconsistent design that stymies recognition? Well, they lose people fast. Simplicity in design, clarity in language, and consistency in presentation create a feeling of ease, which simply and steadily builds confidence.

3. **Emotional Branding**

People don't just buy products—they buy feelings. Nike sells motivation. Apple sells creativity. On a local level, you can powerfully connect to similar emotions. Your brand should aim to evoke a core emotion. Look at the list (from pages 101 – 102) and rally your brand around an emotion that matters. There are plenty of powerful emotions…security, excitement, belonging, empowerment, etc. ...pick yours based on what resonates with your current customer base. Communicate that to the rest of the market and your brand will grow.

4. **Color Psychology**

Colors influence perception. Flip back to pages 47-48 in Chapter 3 for a refresher on the power of color. Here are just a few examples:

- **Blue** = trust, stability (used by banks, tech firms)
- **Red** = energy, urgency (used in sales, fast food)
- **Green** = growth, wellness (used in health, eco-brands)

Choose a color palette aligned with your values and message. Then, stick to it. It's a big component of that brand consistency that I'm always raving about.

5. **Social Proof & Authority**
    Campaigns focused on using the genuine words of others to hype a brand will always be more effective than a brand touting its own greatness.
    Testimonials, case studies, reviews, awards, and endorsements tap into the psychological principle of social validation. People look to others to determine what to trust. Whether it is 'regular people' that they can relate to or a celebrity endorser that they look up to or aspire to emulate, a creative campaign that seeks to build trust in the local market will never go wrong with this approach.

6. **The Mere Exposure Effect**
    Repetition breeds familiarity, and familiarity breeds preference. When people see your brand repeatedly (and consistently), they're more likely to trust it. Years ago, realtors led the way by plastering their faces on everything from business cards to billboards. Sure, the 'can't let go of my ego' jokes rolled, but they tapped nicely into the idea that familiarity brings with it trust and even preference. It's a true and simple formula. The more recognizable your brand is combined with the repetition of exposure, the more trusted your brand will be among consumers.

7. **Scarcity and Urgency**
    Every creative campaign worth its salt will make a strong offer. That offer needs a deadline. Preferably one that creates a tingling sense of urgency with the consumer. Limited-time offers or exclusive access can trigger the fear of missing out (FOMO), prompting quicker decisions. Every campaign is

situational, of course, but any campaign with a deadline longer than 14-days risks losing most consumers…due to procrastination rules alone. Stick to two days to ten days max to spark urgency.

Brand Archetypes: Aligning with Human Motives

I know what you're thinking. How in the world can you talk psychology and branding and NOT mention a great psychologist along the way? Well, the wait is over folks! That's right…because Carl Jung identified 12 universal archetypes—patterns of behavior and symbolism deeply embedded in the human psyche. This is important within the scope of branding because brands that align with an archetype can build stronger identity and truly resonate with their audience. Further, this all happens on an almost exclusively emotional level—where the brand truly resonates.

Here are *Jung's 12 Universal Archetypes* along with a few national brand examples to consider for study in developing your own local brand story:

- **The Hero**: Embodies courage. Determination. Heroes strive to prove their worth through courageous acts. They often face adversity in achieving their goals while protecting others. The brand message is one built on the bravery of a determined protagonist. (Nike, FedEx)
- **The Caregiver**: Represents compassion. Selflessness. Caregivers are nurturing and protective. They are known for putting the needs of others before their own. Ideal for non-profit or health-related brands that need messaging to align

with compassion and nurturing. (Johnson & Johnson, UNICEF)

- **The Explorer**: Symbolizes adventure. Discovery. Explorers seek new experiences and knowledge. Their quests are often never-ending and immersed in a feeling of restlessness. They are constantly on a mission for something new, communicating a sense of adventure and independence. (Jeep, The North Face)
- **The Sage**: Represents wisdom. Knowledge. Sages seek truth and understanding, often guiding others with their insights and experience. They are wise…a thoughtful trusted friend who always seeks to look out for the best interest of others. (Google, Harvard)
- **The Lover**: Embodies passion. Connection. Lovers seek intimacy. They long for deep emotional connections while valuing relationships and appreciating beauty in all forms. (Glamour, Victoria Secrets)
- **The Creator**: Represents innovation. Imagination. Creators are driven by one goal: to express themselves, bringing new ideas to life for all. They often value originality and artistic expression. (Adobe, Lego)
- **The Magician:** Embodies transformation. Change. Magicians long to understand the laws of the universe, seeking to use that knowledge to create change. The brand message within this archetype is grounded in renovation that sparks helpful change through the evolutionary process. (Nvidia, Redwood Materials)
- **The Ruler:** Represents control. Order. Rulers seek to create stability. An authoritative voice that offers instruction, direction and structure. Their brand message is often 'take charge' in nature, ensuring

that their purposeful vision is realized and maintained. (Microsoft, Evernote)
- **Others Include: The Jester; The Orphan; The Innocent; The Rebel**

Choosing an archetype gives your brand a clear personality and emotional tone. And if it connects to your target audience your brand story allows for instant alignment on a deeply meaningful level.

Conclusion

Psychologically, people form relationships with brands much like they do with people. Brands can be seen as trustworthy friends, inspiring mentors, or fun companions. But just like real relationships, trust must be earned over time and can be easily broken. Your brand ignites trust by displaying consistency, transparency...by delivering on promises, time and time again while owning mistakes.

Branding isn't just design—it's psychology in action. By understanding how your audience thinks, feels, and decides, you can shape your brand to connect more deeply and more meaningfully with your audience. When you tap into the power of emotional resonance, simplicity, and human motives, you don't just build a brand—you address Pain Points, and in the process, build loyalty.

Branding psychology is about making sure your audience sees you clearly—warts, wins, and all. Because unlike that Sunday morning, you don't want to wait until the drive-thru for someone to blurt out what everyone else was too polite to say. Better to catch those bloody blind spots early, fix them, and show up with confidence—razor nicks and all.

Chapter 7: Continuity—Branding Across Touchpoints

"Save your money for the moving expenses."

I don't say those words lightly.

It started when one of our account managers asked me to join her for a meeting with a prospective client—a wedding planner who had been open just six months. Before we even sat down with her, I took a look at some of her past marketing pieces. They were all over the place—different fonts, different taglines, images that had nothing to do with each other. No cohesion. No consistency.

When I asked about it, I was told, "Well, she's very creative and doesn't want everything looking the same."

'Creativity' is a wonderful theme to build a brand around—especially for a wedding coordinator. But without continuity? That's a recipe for confusion. And confusion never converts.

So, by the time we met, I had concerns, but what she told us next really painted the picture:

"I've already spent $40,000 on marketing in the last six months and I've got nothing to show for it. I've got to generate $100,000 worth of brides this month, or I'm out."

Dawn, the account manager, leaned in: "So… what do you need from us?"

The wedding planner didn't hesitate, exclaiming: "I need you to save my business!"

"Alright," I said. "What kind of budget are we working with to do that?"

She looked me in the eye and said: "$250."

That's when the words slipped out: "Save your money for the moving expenses."

Because the truth was, her $40,000 hadn't disappeared into thin air. It had been wasted—poured into inconsistent marketing that confused prospects instead of building trust. Consumers on Main Street saw a different **look**, a different **message**, a different **tone** at every touchpoint. There was nothing tying it all together…no cohesive brand ringing true time and time again.

And that's the point: when your branding lacks continuity, you're not just making a design mistake—you're bleeding opportunity. Every disconnected touchpoint chips away at trust until you're left scrambling to "save the business."

Your brand doesn't live in just one place. Every interaction someone has with your business—whether it's your website, packaging, customer service, or even an invoice—shapes their perception of who you are. And when that story doesn't add up, neither will the results. This is why branding must be consistent *across every touchpoint.*

What Are Brand Touchpoints?

A touchpoint is any moment where your customer or prospect interacts with your brand. Think of them as the "little handshakes" your business offers to the outside world. Some are obvious, some are subtle—but they all matter.

When most people think about branding, their mind goes straight to logos and ads. Sure, those are touchpoints. But the truth is, branding is happening in dozens of places you might not even realize. Just a few examples follow:

- **Your website homepage**—does it look current, easy, and helpful—or dated and confusing?
- **Your social media posts**—is there a consistent look, voice, and message…or does every post present a new personality?
- **The flyer on the bulletin board at the local coffee shop**—does it offer consistent design elements with other marketing pieces? (logo, fonts, color scheme)
- **The way your employees answer the phone**—are greetings cheerful and helpful or rushed and annoyed?
- **Even your invoice**—yes, really…your invoice! Does it reinforce professionalism and clarity, or does it look like a quick Word doc with an Arial font?

Each of these touchpoints is an opportunity. Each can either reinforce your brand—or work against it. It is an opportunity to enhance the brand's relationship with the customer or detract from it. And here's the kicker: you don't get to choose which ones people notice. A customer might remember your friendly Facebook response but also the messy lobby that prompted a quick eye roll. In their mind, it all adds up to who you are as a brand.

Back to the 'manila folder of the mind' metaphor—each touchpoint means opening that folder and stuffing it with something. Some good. Some bad. And for local businesses especially, every touchpoint carries extra weight. In a smaller market, word travels faster and impressions stick longer. People notice. And because your brand lives in their community—not just on a national screen—each touchpoint is a chance to either strengthen trust or quietly erode it.

So, when we talk about branding across touchpoints, we're not just talking about "marketing." We're talking about every corner of the business where someone bumps into your brand and walks away with a perception.

Brand touchpoints can be physical, digital, or experiential. Here is a more conclusive list of these opportunities to keep an eye on:

Common Examples Include:

- Printed Materials: Business Cards, Brochures, Rack Cards, Posters, Folders, etc.
- Storefront appearance, including POS displays
- Employee Uniforms
- Email communications
- Promotional Products—having a signature giveaway item that consumers crave is gold!
- Packaging and product design
- Advertising (digital, print, TV, outdoor)
- Customer support interactions
- Invoices and proposals
- Retail environments or office space

- Events, trade shows, or webinars

Each touchpoint is an opportunity to reinforce your brand—or dilute it. Take advantage!

Why Consistency Matters

I'm a big baseball fan—specifically a long-time supporter of the New York Yankees. I'm pretty old school in my sports mindset and love how my Yanks have two uniforms: The Pinstripe Home Unis with the signature NY and the gray Road set with the block letter 'NEW YORK'. Many teams have many, many combinations, which is bad enough to this old school dude. But imagine if the Yanks took the field in completely mismatched uniforms. One player's wearing orange, another in purple, another in a throwback jersey. They may all be talented athletes, but do they look like a team? Nope. Consistency is what tells the world, "We belong together. We're united. You can trust us."

This is true in baseball. And true with your brand as well. If your website says one thing, your Facebook ads another, and your employees yet another, prospects don't know which "team" they're dealing with. Confusion sets in. And, I'll say it again—here's the bottom line reality:

☞ **Confused customers never buy.**

Consistency isn't about making everything look identical—it is about making everything feel like it comes from the same place, delivered by the same voice, making the same promise. Congruency lands with consumers, whereas a lack of it confuses. The former causes the consumer to **lean in**...the latter creates the opposite effect.

When your brand is consistent across touchpoints:

- **Trust grows faster.** People know what to expect from you.
- **Memorability increases.** The more often someone sees or hears a unified message, the more likely that it sticks.
- **Your marketing dollars stretch further.** Ads reinforce each other instead of essentially competing with each other.
- **Employees align better.** A shared playbook keeps the whole team on-brand.

Back to our wedding planner story—her problem wasn't a lack of creativity. Not at all—she was an incredibly talented and imaginative pro. The issue was that every single touchpoint told a different story. One ad screamed "glamour." Another whispered "discount." Another had no clear voice at all. To prospects, it looked like three or four different businesses fighting for attention against each other. That's why $40,000 disappeared without results. There was no unified brand for anyone to grab hold of.

Consistency, on the other hand, is what makes your brand believable. It reassures the customer that what you say on Monday will still be true next Friday. That what they saw online matches what they experience in person. It's the glue that holds your brand relationship together.

Branding is about trust. If you look different or sound different every time, customers can't even pin down who you are. Much less connect with your brand. Inconsistent branding confuses people. Consistency, on the other hand:

- Builds **trust** through familiarity
- Enhances **brand recall**
- Reinforces your brand's **message and values**
- Increases **conversion rates** by creating a seamless experience

Imagine encountering a sleek, luxury-themed Instagram feed for a skincare brand—clicking for more info only to reach a cluttered website full of typos that doesn't even mention the product. That disconnect weakens the brand's credibility…while creating a certain 'fail to sale' effect.

Think back to Chapter 6 regarding psychology (page 96) and the analogy of the friend who changes their personality every time you meet them. Hard to trust, right? Sure. That sought-after trust builds touchpoint by touchpoint and if elements are continually slipping through the cracks so does the brand. The manila folder fills up with incoherent drivel because that's what the consumer knows about you.

On the other hand, consistency builds familiarity. Familiarity builds loyalty. Consumers should be able to look at your marketing pieces and be able to identify you— **even without a logo**. That's how much continuity should be built-in to your brand. Because even without that major brand identifier, consumers can fall back on a similar voice and personality, consistent fonts for headlines, sub-heads and text and visual imagery.

What Inconsistency Really Costs You

The cost of delivering an inconsistent message to Main Street is hefty. We've seen it already with the wedding planner, right? It was a business that needed more than mere word of mouth to thrive. A great concept that eventually fell flat because the marketing execution was a moving target thanks to a constant shift in messaging. The result? A brand that had potential—but no stability. And without consistency, stability never shows up.

Make no mistake: inconsistency has a price tag. A big one.

Take a local plumber. If you're sending out crews that have mismatched uniforms…a few billboards around town that all shout different messages…and a website and leave behind brochures that look like they could belong to a different company altogether, well, you're not building a brand—you're building confusion. And confusion always sends customers running in the other direction.

Here's what inconsistency really costs you:

> - **Money wasted**… ads, flyers, and posts that don't connect.
> - **Confused customers**…"Wait, is this the same company?"
> - **Missed word-of-mouth**…customers truly don't know how to stuff that manila folder in their mind—or describe you to their neighbors.

When working with a new account, that vital element of consistency is one of the first things we examine. We look at every touchpoint and look for congruency. We see if every marketing piece passes the ole **logo cover up test**: simply cover up the logo and ask yourself, 'can you still identify this brand from the other elements in the ad?' If the answer is no, you've got work to do.

🔊 *True Story*...A community bank we worked with ran holiday TV spots that were basically blooper reels from the year's shoots. Fun? Absolutely. Lighthearted? You bet. But recognizable? Not so much. Without clear brand anchors— like colors, typography, or a voice that carried through— those ads could've been from any bank. Sure, part of financial institution advertising is prompting current customers to feel confident in their choice. That segment might've recognized a familiar face, but for everyone else, it looked like a brand-new institution.

The solution wasn't to scrap the idea. Rather, it was to tie the fun back to the brand. A few well-placed brand cues turned those "funny clips" into brand **recognizable** funny clips. Suddenly the ads carried both personality and consistency. And that's the point: consistency doesn't kill creativity—it fuels it.

Inconsistency is like a leaky pipe. You may not notice the drip at first, but left unchecked, it can cost you a fortune. Tighten it up, and you don't just stop the leak—you build pressure behind a strong, recognizable brand that customers can trust.

Mapping the Customer Journey

If consistency is the glue of branding, the customer journey is the map that shows you where that glue needs to hold everything together. Every prospect or customer goes through a series of interactions—big and small—that collectively shape how they feel about your brand.

Think of it like planning a road trip. You wouldn't just hop in the car and hope for the best (well, maybe in college I did that, but not now). No. You would map out the route, plan stops, and make sure the whole trip feels smooth. Your customers expect the same level of thoughtfulness in their journey with your business.

Creating a specific and detailed 'map' of the consumer's journey with your brand helps you iron out potential issues before they become major pit stops and serve to push you toward brand consistency.

A typical customer journey touches:

- **Awareness** – The moment they discover you (social media ad, Google search, word of mouth).
- **Consideration** – Checking you out (website visit, reading reviews, walking past your storefront).
- **Decision** – Taking the leap (making a purchase, scheduling a consultation, signing a contract).
- **Experience** – Living with that choice (using your product, working with your team, attending your event).
- **Loyalty & Advocacy** – Coming back, telling friends, leaving glowing reviews.

At each stage, your job is to keep the brand voice clear, consistent, and emotionally relevant. After all, the **Awareness** and **Consideration** stages could involve numerous touchpoints. In the 90's, the number of ad impressions you needed to motivate a consumer lingered around **3x per week**. In the first decade of the 2000's? Try **7x per week**. Now? It varies by industry, of course, but that number can reach **3-5x per day**! That could mean multiple impressions made by streaming ads, which eventually lead a prospect to your social media which in turn prompts a click to your website for purchase.

Now imagine if each touchpoint is incongruent from the previous. That search could come to a screeching halt, right! But what if one touchpoint leads to the next with solid consistency in presentation and voice? Well, then you are literally helping the consumer move into the **Decision** phase of their journey with great confidence. From there, it is merely taking care of them through the final stages and welcoming them into the brand's family of advocates.

Let's look at one at an example from one of my favorites— a local donut and coffee shop:

- **Awareness:** A social media ad promises "Cozy mornings, crafted one cup at a time."
- **Consideration:** Their website highlights fresh donuts served with warm community vibes, friendly service, and artisan brews…along with a reminder to bring the kids by Saturday morning for free donut holes!
- **Decision:** The in-store experience matches the promise—friendly baristas greet you by name…asking you if you want the 'usual' as the décor feels warm and consistent with the previous marketing touchpoints.
- **Experience:** The donuts? Amazing! And the coffee delivers, too—rich, fresh, worth the price.
- **Loyalty & Advocacy:** You snap a photo of your latte art and post it, becoming an unpaid brand ambassador.

If even one of those touchpoints felt disconnected—say, the ad promised cozy mornings but the shop felt cold and rushed—the trust cracks. A single gap can turn a great journey into a dead end.

Keep in mind, one misstep may not spark disaster for the brand. If you have plenty of brand equity amassed with the customer, a single misstep may go virtually unnoticed. But for the new customer? Well, it's far more glaring; and new customers are far less forgiving.

The takeaway? When you map your customer journey, you're creating a dry run tailored to your brand experience. In the process, you reveal the cracks before your customers do. And once you see the cracks, you can align every touchpoint to tell one clear, compelling story. That creates a big win for those newbies, and even those with which you've built plenty of brand equity.

Aligning Messaging Across Touchpoints

Once you've mapped your customer journey, the next step is ensuring your brand speaks with one voice at every stage. Inconsistent messaging is like having a band where the horns play jazz, the guitarist shreds metal, while the singer croons country ballads about their dog driving their neighbor's pickup truck. Each might be talented on their own, but together? Eh…Chaos.

Consistency doesn't mean being boring—it means being recognizable. It means creating the warmth of familiarity. It adds up to an "Ah, this is the ticket" reaction from your customer. Whether they're scrolling your Instagram, opening your email, calling your customer service number, or standing in your store, they know through that familiarity that it is a place they belong.

Here are some ways to align messaging across touchpoints:

1. Define Your Core Message

Your brand message should clearly answer: Who do you serve? What problem do you solve and what Pain Points are addressed? Why does it matter? This becomes the anchor. Everything else—from taglines to sales scripts—should connect back to this.

2. Create a Brand Voice Guide

Are you warm and conversational? Professional and precise? Quirky and fun? Lock in your brand personality and share examples with your team so emails, ads, social posts, and even customer support chats "sound" like the same brand. This helps everyone speak with that same voice and that is key to building a successful brand experience.

3. Visual Continuity Matters Too

Fonts, colors, logo placement, image styles—all need to line up. A strong design system ensures your brochure matches your website, your social graphics match your signage, and nothing feels "off brand."

4. Audit Your Messaging Regularly

Walk through your own customer journey once a quarter. Pretend you're a new prospect. Does your messaging still feel consistent from the first click to the last invoice? If not, fix it. Next, run through the same exercise as an existing customer. Does that same brand voice still ring loud and clear touchpoint to touchpoint?

5. Train Your Team

Every employee is a brand ambassador. If your marketing promises "fast, friendly service," but your receptionist sounds rushed and irritated, the entire brand promise breaks. Alignment isn't just about words on paper—it's about behavior in practice.

For instance, one of our clients in the financial sector positioned themselves as "neighbors helping neighbors." Their website reflected it, their ads reflected it, but Mystery Shopping revealed interactions more aligned with "neighbors battling neighbors". Shoppers reported employees being confrontational about simple questions with cold, distant and robotic engagement.

We were wasting money promoting a brand that was not being lived across the board. But once we went through a **Brand**TRAINING session that taught the team to match the neighborly tone, behavior shifted dramatically. There was friction initially. After all, people are people—and people get 'stuck' in their ways, right! All of that was overcome once the employees understood the 'why' behind the 'what'. This put everyone on the same page and furthered the brand greatly. Another round of Mystery Shopping verified that prospective customers stopped seeing them as "just another bank" and started seeing them as a trusted partner.

The bottom line: getting everyone on the same page helps the **brand align in order to build trust**. And in business, trust always comes before transactions.

Tools for Consistency

We've established that consistency is the glue holding your brand together across touchpoints. But you can't just "hope" for consistency. Hope isn't a strategy. You need tools and systems that make consistency automatic—even when multiple people (or entire teams) are creating marketing, customer service replies, or sales collateral.

Here are some practical tools every business can put in place:

1. Brand Design System

Think of this as your brand's rulebook. It outlines your logo usage, color palette complete with CMYK, RGB and Pantone Matching System coding, typography, imagery style, and messaging framework. Every designer, copywriter, and staff member should have access to it. Even if you're a small business, a 10-page guideline beats relying on memory or "eh…it's close enough!"

2. Marketing Calendar

"If you fail to plan, you plan to fail." It was the favorite saying of a co-worker. It was also a true and wise tidbit of advice. Creating a Marketing Calendar doesn't just keep you organized; it ensures your voice and themes stay consistent over time. Plan campaigns and every marketing platform you will utilize within it, including social media posts, email blasts, and promotions. And…keep it all in one place so you can see if each campaign reinforces (or contradicts) each other.

3. Message Map

This simple chart lays out your core message, supporting points, and proof examples. This keeps all communications, from your sales rep's elevator pitch and website copy to customer conversations and social media replies, all speaking from the same playbook.

4. Template Library

Flyers, proposals, presentations, social graphics—all branded, pre-approved, and ready for customization. This prevents "rogue marketing" where someone slaps your logo onto a random design and calls it good enough.

5. Employee Training Sessions

We call it **BrandTRAINING**, but regardless of how you reference it, create a program that recognizes your employees as true and valued brand ambassadors. Refresher courses on what the brand is all about and how it is to be lived daily is a strong way to, not only reinvigorate a team, but give them the tools to make the brand come to life. A regularly scheduled (annually, bi-annually or quarterly) revitalization session ensures your team knows how to live out the brand day-to-day. Make it fun. Feed them. Give away some gift cards. All while reinforcing to them how to bring the brand to life—think role-playing customer calls, daily do's and don'ts.

6. Regular Audits

Set aside time (every six months, minimum) to do a brand audit. Check your touchpoints: Does your website messaging align with your social posts? Do your ads reflect your tagline? Do your customer service emails still sound like "you"? This closes the gaps and helps manage consistency before trust is damaged.

I get it. It can seem a smidge overwhelming. Start small. Even a simple three-tool combo (design system + message map + marketing calendar) can transform a business's consistency.

🔊 *True Story*... An HVAC client struggled with mismatched door hangers, ads, and social media posts—every piece looked like it came from a different company. They asked us to unify the brand into a cohesive unit. We did so by building a Brand Template Library and Marketing Calendar. Then, everything "snapped into place." They didn't just look more like the pros they were, but reported fewer confused calls ("Wait, are you the guys that...?") and more qualified leads that trusted them from the start.

At the end of the day, consistency isn't just about looking polished. That's great, but it's about more. It's about making it easy for people to recognize, trust, and choose you again and again, which is what local branding is all about.

Conclusion: Consistency Is Trust

Branding across touchpoints is about making sure every single interaction reinforces the same story. Every time someone encounters your brand—whether on a billboard, a website, a business card, or a face-to-face conversation—they're unconsciously asking themselves, "Can I trust this?" Consistency is what leads them to an affirmative answer. It reassures customers that what they see is what they'll get, no matter the touchpoint.

Inconsistency? Well, on the other hand, incongruity sends subtle signals of disorganization and unreliability. It's like someone who changes their story every time you talk to them—you'd hesitate to invest heavily in that relationship, right? Brands are no different. When your message, tone, visuals, and service all align across every interaction, your brand identity moves from an abstract concept to a living, breathing and genuine experience.

Tools, such as a Brand Design System and a Marketing Calendar, can help enforce your brand's consistency. Your people, properly trained, can carry it forward. But at the heart of it, branding across touchpoints is about building trust through sameness. And trust, once established, becomes the most powerful currency your brand will ever hold.

Consistency across every touchpoint is what builds trust, recognition, and loyalty. But there's a twist. In today's world, many of those touchpoints aren't physical signs, billboards, or brochures—they're digital. That means the challenge of space limitations...seconds to relay a first and lasting impression and so much more. A customer may form their very first impression of your brand by scrolling your Instagram feed, landing on your website, or reading an online review. That means your brand has to live and breathe just as strongly online as it does on Main Street. In the next chapter, we'll explore what it really takes to build a brand in the digital era—and how to make sure your identity translates seamlessly from storefront to smartphone.

Chapter 8: Branding in the Digital Era

Yes, I'm risking sounding very old school here, but just a few decades ago, a local business could thrive on a simple recipe. Take good curb appeal, mix in a clean storefront, and add a friendly smile at the counter—with maybe a dash of seasoning like a steady local newspaper ad, a Yellow Pages ad and sponsoring a Little League team. That was enough to get people through the door and keep 'em coming back.

But today? The first impression doesn't usually happen when someone steps inside—it happens when they type your biz into Google or stumble across your social feed.

I'll never forget working with a local florist right as the internet was taking shape as a real marketing tool. He had a great store, great staff, and a wide variety of flowers for every occasion. What he didn't have was a digital presence. His frustration was simple: "Everyone is calling those 1-800 numbers…and we've got no margins using those services; or worse…people are going online and I'm not messing with that."

The biggest obstacle to getting him profitable again wasn't competition—it was his refusal to embrace the digital realm. Not because he thought it was a passing fad, but because he wanted to bury his head in the tulips and hope it would all go away.

The result? It didn't go away. Unfortunately, the store did. We threw everything at it—great TV and radio campaigns, loyalty programs, community sponsorships. But ultimately, it wasn't enough. Because the one thing needed most—a digital footprint—was the one thing we weren't allowed to create. That online presence could have opened new audiences, added revenue streams, and created a community of customers who stuck with him.

And folks, that was 25 years ago. Back then, the internet was still just an "option." Today? It's oxygen. Social media, SEO, paid search, CTV/OTT, retargeting—all are part of the playing field.

That's the world we live in: digital first impressions now make or break your brand before you ever get a chance to arrange a bouquet, shake a hand, or tell your story. And while the tools and platforms may change, the principles of branding do not. The challenge today isn't convincing people to look up from the tulips—it's ensuring your timeless brand identity shows up as clearly online as it does in person.

Simply put: in today's world, your brand almost always meets its audience online first.

Why Digital is Different — But Not Separate

It's tempting to think of "digital marketing" as some shiny new toy—separate from your core brand strategy. Many local business owners fall into this trap. They'll say, "We've got our brand over here, and then we've got our internet stuff over there. We'll use an agency for the 'real advertising,' but my daughter has a lot of Facebook fans so she can do our social media and my nephew can whip up a website."

That thinking is dangerous.

My niece has sparkling white teeth, but she's not my dentist. (She is a trained hair stylist, and yes, she has cut my hair—see the difference?) Every marketing touchpoint—whether it's a billboard, a business card, or your Facebook feed—has to be treated with the same level of seriousness. They all communicate your brand, and if one piece is sloppy or even slightly off-brand, the whole picture suffers.

Digital isn't separate from your brand. It's simply the newest, most visible set of touchpoints where your brand shows up. Just as your storefront signage, your invoices, and even your voicemail greeting communicate who you are, so do your website, your Instagram feed, your email newsletter, and your Google reviews.

The difference with digital? **Speed and scale.**

- A bad in-store experience might turn off one person and even spread to a few within their circle of friends. A negative online review? That can sour thousands.
- A well-crafted Facebook post can create word-of-mouth at lightning speed, spreading in ways a newspaper ad never could.
- And unlike a billboard or radio spot, digital touchpoints can shift in real time. You can update a headline, tweak an image, or adjust a call-to-action almost instantly.

Keep in mind, I'm not 'slamming' other media. At
BrandVision Marketing, we have worked with just about
every media. (Except those ads on urinals—no brand
should pay to get peed on!) Each media has strengths. Each
has weaknesses. Simply put: We work with what will best
accomplish a client's goal within their budget. But what
I'm talking about here is the ability to scale, and fast.
Digital can be a big winner along those lines.

Actually, it can be a powerful tool. But it also comes with
risks. Because inconsistency, sloppiness, or ignoring your
digital presence isn't just a missed opportunity—it's a
liability.

Think of digital like a microphone. It amplifies what's
already there. If your brand is clear and consistent, digital
tools carry that clarity further, faster, and more effectively.
That's a mic drop. If your brand is muddled? Digital just
makes the confusion louder—and that's reverb.

**Digital branding isn't a new game—it's the same game
played at higher speed with a potentially bigger
audience.** The principles of distinction, relevance and
consistency, don't change. What changes is the urgency
and visibility.

Translating Branding Elements into Digital

Remember those core seven elements of your brand
identity from Chapter 3—logo, color palette, typography,
imagery, tagline, voice, and design system? Their job was
to build a consistent presence in the physical world. They
serve to bring the brand to life, right?

How do those same elements translate into digital touchpoints? Here's the answer: **directly**. If your brand identity is the DNA, digital platforms are simply another body for it to live in.

1. **Logo** – Your logo needs to scale cleanly from a tiny profile icon on Instagram to a banner on your website. That means using simplified versions when needed (favicon, social avatar) but always keeping the core mark intact. If people can't recognize you at thumbnail size, you've got a problem.

2. **Color Palette** – Digital is unforgiving if you're inconsistent. HEX Codes, not just "that shade of blue," are your friend. What is a HEX Code? Good question. A hex code is a way to match colors in digital design (specifically your website). This six-character string of letters and numbers specifies the intensity of red, green, and blue in a color. They are widely used to define colors for various elements on a web page. Whether it's your website button, your email header, or your LinkedIn banner, consistent colors make the scroll-stopping difference. Be aware of yours.

3. **Typography** – Fonts may look great in print but fall apart online. Choose web-friendly families that reflect your personality without killing legibility. A boutique that insists on script fonts for everything? Cute, until nobody can read the menu on their phone. Determine the web-friendlies from the web-enemies before you pick your typography.

4. **Imagery** – This is where many local brands either shine or stumble. Skip the generic stock photos of "business people shaking hands." Instead, use authentic, high-quality shots of your team with your customers in your community. Digital audiences crave real.

5. **Tagline** – Your tagline becomes especially powerful online. It's a voice of competitive separation living in an arena of fellow gladiators—serving to give you the needed weapon to win the sale. But it's not just under the logo—it's the one-liner in your social media bio, the anchor in your website header, the closing line in your YouTube outro. Keep it short, punchy, and consistent.

6. **Voice and Tone** – This is your biggest digital differentiator. Every caption, tweet, or email is a chance to sound like you—not like a corporate bot. If your brand is friendly and neighborly, your posts should sound like a conversation, not a press release. Have more of a professional tone? Forget the cheesy humor and stick to the facts. Know your voice and be on-brand…consistently.

7. **Design System** – Online, this is where you protect yourself. A digital style guide ensures that your daughter running Facebook and an outsourced vendor designing Google ads are using the same fonts, colors, tone, and templates. Consistency across platforms makes your brand instantly recognizable no matter where someone encounters you.

The point is simple: your brand's digital presence shouldn't feel like a different version of your brand. It's not a spin-off series—it's the same story, same characters, just showing up on a different screen.

🔊 *True Story*…Remember how BrandVision Marketing created that tagline "Welcome Home" to serve as a meaningful competitive differentiator for a local community bank? We chose that specific font for multiple reasons. Yes, Cooper Black features thick letterforms with soft curves, making it very legible and big-time impactful. Yes, its warm, friendly appearance lends itself nicely to use in various branding and advertising contexts. All tolled? It really hit the mark, right! But all would have fallen short on that selection if it was not web-friendly. It is. Cooper Black is generally considered a website-friendly font due to its bold and rounded serif design, which checked every box for display to use across platforms:

Website...✔

Social Media...✔

Banner Ads...✔

That made Cooper Black the ultimate pick. I've seen plenty of clients pick fonts because they like the look. That's great; and I get it. But that look needs to translate—from the tangible (i.e. brochures and business cards) to the digital space, too.

The Power of Digital Touchpoints

Think of every place your brand shows up digitally as a "touchpoint"—a moment where someone interacts with you, forms an impression, and prompts the consumer to open that 'manila folder of the mind'. Simply put: They decide whether to move closer to your brand or further away. The sheer power of digital branding lies in how many of these moments you now have and how fast they multiply.

In the "old days," a customer might see your sign, your print ad, and maybe your TV spot before stepping inside. Today, the digital journey is vastly different:

1) They Google you.
2) They see your Google Reviews and star rating.
3) They scan your website.
4) They peek at your social media to "get a more personal feel" for you.
5) They notice your streaming ad on Facebook, YouTube or Hulu.
6) They get retargeted with another ad after visiting your site.
7) And only then…maybe…do they walk through your door.

That's right. The process is suddenly ripe with extra steps to provoke action. It can get complicated. Every single one of those touchpoints is a chance to win trust—or lose it. And here's the kicker: they all work together. A slick website can be undone by a few bad Yelp reviews. A friendly Facebook ad loses credibility if the landing page feels cold or confusing.

Digital magnifies both the good and the bad.

> **A positive touchpoint** (a glowing testimonial video, a helpful blog post, or a warm response to a comment) can ripple outward—shared, liked, and remembered…as the brand builds that 'manila folder of the mind' in an encouraging light.
> **A negative touchpoint** (a broken link, a snarky reply, or a dated design) can spread just as quickly, leaving scars on your reputation…filling that manila folder with undesirable thoughts.

That's why consistency isn't just a "nice to have." It's survival. Digital touchpoints are like dominoes: line them up carefully, and one good impression neatly falls into another until you've built momentum. Line them up sloppily? Well, then one poorly placed domino sends the whole thing crashing down before that positive energy builds.

📢 *True Story*... When working with a personal injury attorney, the firm valued the idea of "having a web presence," but the execution? Well, it was all over the place. The website logo was stretched beyond recognition and didn't match the one used in digital ads or TV spots. Social media? Totally different typography, colors, and tone. Every touchpoint looked like it came from a different law firm.

Once we gained access to their platforms, we streamlined everything—logos, fonts, and even the messaging tone. Suddenly, the entire brand felt cohesive, professional, and recognizable.

Had that inconsistency hurt their earlier campaigns? Hard to quantify exactly, though new cases saw a clear uptick afterward. What's certain is this: the upside of continuity is undeniable. You may look at two slightly different versions of your logo and know it's the same company. Most consumers won't. To them, it's two companies competing for attention. And that, my friends, is a big "uh-oh."

Digital touchpoints give local businesses more leverage than ever before—especially when it comes to growth.

Many local businesses still rely on word-of-mouth, which traditionally meant a neighbor telling three friends. That's great—your brand lives inside that person's small social circle. But today, one positive interaction can be screenshotted, shared, and seen by thousands before lunch.

That's the difference between old-school word-of-mouth and modern digital amplification. Word-of-mouth might influence three to ten prospects. A well-crafted campaign, on the other hand, can reach thousands and attract a hundred interested leads. Even with a modest 30% close ratio, that's three new customers versus thirty. That's not theory—that's **bottom-line** impact.

And that's the real power of digital touchpoints: they scale your brand message faster—and farther—than any billboard, and yes, word-of-mouth, ever could. The only question is: are they scaling the right story?

Pitfalls to Avoid in the Digital Era

If you've read this far…and you have, right? **Right!?** Well, then you already know that digital branding is full of opportunity — but it's a realm also full of traps. Like walking through a digital minefield wearing clown shoes. The landscape moves fast, platforms evolve overnight, and the temptation to chase the next shiny thing is so real.

Below are some of the most common pitfalls we see local brands fall into, and more importantly, how you can avoid them.

1. Treating Digital Like an Afterthought

Some business owners still see digital as the "extra credit" of marketing — nice to have if you can fit it in. They'll spend thousands on signage, radio, or sponsorships but won't invest in the same level of strategy or creativity online. The reality? For many consumers, your digital presence **is** your storefront. It's where first impressions are made, trust is built, and decisions happen.

According to a CapitalOne Shopping survey*[1], most consumers experience a hybrid of the **online to brick-and-mortar experience**. The ratio of consumers who visit a website versus those who visit the same business' brick-and-mortar store varies, but the stats are clear:

> ➤ 43% of consumers prefer online shopping, while 45% prefer in-store shopping.
> ➤ 45% of consumers visit stores for the convenience of in-person shopping.
> ➤ 29% of consumers shop both online and in-store, indicating a preference for both methods.

We see a distinct overlap in shopping habits, with many consumers relying on both online and in-person shopping options. With that in mind, skimping in the digital arena would be a big whiff.

☞ **Fix:** Give your digital touchpoints the same strategic weight as your traditional ones. Think of them as partners, not sidekicks.

2. Inconsistency across Channels

We've covered this a bit, but it's worth repeating because it's one of the biggest killers of brand equity. The second your Facebook page says one thing and your website says another, confusion begins. And confusion kills conversions.

☞ **Fix:** Audit your touchpoints regularly. Make sure your logo, tone, typography, and calls-to-action are aligned.

3. Talking At Your Audience Instead of With Them

The old broadcast mindset dies hard. Some brands still shout promotions into the void, forgetting that digital is a two-way conversation. People don't want to be lectured — they want to be engaged, heard, and occasionally entertained. Even through CTV ads, which is essentially the TV ad experience on a streaming device, brands can use QR Codes and more as a way to further the conversation. Remember, **engage** don't preach.

☞ **Fix:** Create content that invites response. Ask questions, share user stories, and show up in the comments like a real human (not a corporate monolith).

4. Ignoring the Data

One of digital's greatest gifts is measurability. Yet too many brands fly blind, never checking analytics or tracking conversions. That's like paying for billboard space but never putting up the ad.

☞ **Fix:** Don't worry about tracking everything. Track what matters — engagement, click-throughs, conversions, and retention. Yes, you can forget about the vanity stats— unless you need an occasional pick-me-up. Focus on what matters and then act on the insights.

5. Chasing Every Trend

From TikTok dances to AI everything, it's easy to get caught up in whatever's hot this week. But not every trend fits your brand — and some will do more harm than good. Remember: relevance beats novelty every time. Live where your customers live and commit to those platforms. Assess the cost of true engagement with that latest shiny toy and see if its ROI is up to snuff.

☞ **Fix:** Ask, "Does this align with who we are and who we serve?" If not, skip it. Your brand shouldn't have an identity crisis just to stay "current."

6. Forgetting the Human Touch

Automation is amazing — until it makes you sound like a robot. Whether it's auto-replies, chatbots, or templated posts, don't let convenience cost you connection. If you're on LinkedIn you smell the auto-replies a mile away, right?

"Thank you for posting such insightful information. It is refreshing to see such progressive ideas in motion. Keep up the good work!"

Come on! C3-PO had far more personality, right? Be genuine in your engagement. These are real people looking for sincere connection with your brand. Deliver that.

☞ **Fix:** Use automation smartly, but always add a personal touch. A brand that feels human will always outshine one that just feels efficient.

7. Not Protecting Your Rep

Online reviews are today's word-of-mouth—only faster, louder, and far more public. Too many businesses ignore or mishandle them until it's too late. We've all had whiffs in this category. It's human nature to put up a defense shield when you feel under attack. I get it. But silence or defensiveness online doesn't make you look classy; it makes you look guilty.

The same goes for complaints made directly to your customer service team. When a customer comes at you with figurative guns-a-blazin', do this: agree with them. That's right—on some level, agree with them. Show empathy and understanding, even if you can't give them everything they want. Nothing diffuses anger faster than agreement— making an upset customer feeling heard and validated.

What doesn't work? The canned corporate response. You know the one:

> *"We at AT&T value your business and would never do anything to disrupt your trust..."*

Are you kidding me? That's how big brands talk because they've resigned themselves to being disliked. But on Main Street, it needs to be different. It needs to be human.

So when it comes to reviews, let your customers see that you care. Acknowledge their frustration, fix the issue if you can, and show a little personality. Empathy and honesty go a long way toward turning a negative into a glowing win in that manila folder of the mind.

☞ **Fix:** Monitor reviews consistently, respond professionally, and view criticism as a gift. Every reply is a chance to demonstrate your brand's values. Each interaction is an opportunity to enhance—or detract from— the brand. Deliver the former.

🔊 *True Story*...Digital pitfalls can be avoided and certainly fixed. A few years back, BrandVision Marketing began working with a local motorsports dealer (ATVs/UTVs) that had hit the gas on digital—but in many ways found itself stuck in a ditch. They had a decent traditional brand presence, but their online identity? Well, it was a total split personality. Their Google ads were loud and pushy while their Facebook posts were sentimental quotes about "family fun," and the website? Well, it hadn't been updated since the Bush administration—the first one. (Yeah...okay that's an exaggeration but it needed work!)

The confusion didn't just hurt engagement. It hurt trust. When we reviewed their analytics, their SEO was in-line, the click-through rate from paid search looked fine, but conversions were as scary as tanking from a trail's rut only to look up at Sasquatch staring you down. People were landing on the site, taking one look, and bailing fast. You know that old motorsports saying, "Life is better in the mud"? Well, that's pretty much where the site was stuck.

So, we cleaned it up. Unified the message. Gave every digital touchpoint the same tone, color scheme, and confidence. In less than 90 days, their conversion rate jumped 47%. More sales appointments. More service appointments. And a growing list of email newsletter subscribers. No new gimmicks, no new trends, just good, old-fashioned brand consistency adapted to a digital world.

The moral? The tools didn't fail them—the **inconsistency** did. Digital doesn't require you to reinvent who you are. It just requires you to show up the same way everywhere you appear.

The digital space can make or break your brand faster than ever before. But with awareness, consistency, and a bit of humility, you can navigate it like a pro. After all, you don't know that Sasquatch wants to hurt you…he may just want to borrow your UTV. So, remember — the goal isn't perfection—it's progress. The brands that win in the digital era aren't the ones that never make mistakes; they're the ones that learn, adapt, and stay true to who they are through every pixel, post, and click.

The Digital Era Advantage

You're probably noticing a theme here. That is: the digital world can be a brand's best friend or its worst enemy. It all depends on how you show up.

But here's the beautiful part — when you get it right, the digital era isn't a threat at all. It's the greatest branding advantage local businesses have ever had.

In decades past, getting your message to the masses required a media budget that rivaled a national brand's. Not today. The playing field is flatter than ever. The digital era gives local brands something they never had before: reach, precision, and accountability. For decades, small businesses had to rely on broad-stroke advertising—print, radio, billboards—hoping the right person saw or heard the message. Today, you can talk directly to your ideal customer, right where they live, scroll, and spend time online.

That's powerful.

You no longer have to outspend the competition—you just have to outthink them.

With the right digital tools, local brands can look, sound, and perform like industry giants — even on a Main Street budget. Harness that strategically and here's what you get:

- ✓ **Precision Targeting:** You no longer have to hope the right people see your ad. Platforms like CTV/OTT, Google Ads, and Meta let you zero in on exactly who you want — by behavior, location, interest, or need. You're not shouting into the void and only praying someone is there; no—you're having a one-on-one conversation with someone ready to listen…right on Main Street.
- ✓ **Real-Time Feedback:** Traditional advertising can still contribute to your strategy, but it is a waiting game. Digital gives you instant feedback — impressions, clicks, conversions — data you can adjust to optimize performance in real time. When used right, that feedback loop becomes your secret weapon.
- ✓ **Scalability:** Digital lets you test, measure, and scale what works. No guesswork. No waste. That's not just marketing efficiency — it's marketing accountability…something long absent in the world of traditional advertising.
- ✓ **Authentic Connection:** The most powerful brands don't just talk at their audiences; they interact with them. Social media, email marketing, and video storytelling make that possible 24/7 — giving even small brands the chance to build deep, lasting relationships with their communities, which is what branding is all about.

It's not about mastering every shiny new platform or chasing the latest algorithm tweak. It's about bringing the same brand consistency, clarity, and confidence you've built offline into every digital interaction.

That's the real digital advantage: it's not just your message that travels faster — it's your brand essence.

And if this feels like a lot to manage, you're not wrong. The opportunities are endless, but they need a system — a framework that connects the strategy dots between branding and digital execution.

That's where *Digital Marketing Blueprint: A Strategic Guide to Achieving Measurable Results* steps in. It is the companion to this book and details an eight-step process for building a measurable, accountable digital strategy that amplifies your brand instead of diluting it. From setting smart goals to defining your funnel, tracking results, and optimizing campaigns, it's your roadmap for bringing the same discipline and focus to your digital marketing that you've built into your brand itself.

Branding builds the foundation. It's who you are, what you stand for, and how you make people feel.

Digital marketing is the megaphone. It's how you deliver that message to the right people, in the right place, at the right time.

When both work together—solid branding paired with smart digital strategy—you've got a force multiplier. Because branding and digital marketing are not separate conversations. They're two sides of the same coin — and when you bring them together, that's when your business really starts to shine.

The digital era hasn't made branding obsolete—it's made it essential. Because in a world where every click, view, and scroll is an opportunity to connect, your brand is no longer just what people see.

It's what they **feel**, what they **share**, and ultimately—what they **remember**.

Conclusion

Branding is timeless. Digital has simply leveled the playing field—putting Main Street businesses on the world's biggest stage.

Digital branding isn't just about being online—it's about how you show up online. Those seven core brand identity elements we discussed in Chapter 3—logo, color palette, typography, imagery, tagline, voice, and design system— must carry over seamlessly into the digital space. This continuity is what ensures that when customers move between your physical and digital touchpoints, they never lose sight of who you are.

The brands that thrive in the digital era are clear, consistent, responsive, and human. They connect, listen, and adapt— without ever abandoning their values, voice, or personality.

The digital age has completely transformed how brands are built and perceived. In a world where content spreads in seconds and attention is the scarcest currency of all, your online presence isn't just part of your brand—it is your brand.

Whether you're a new startup or legacy cash cow, your digital touchpoints are now your first and most frequent interactions with your audience.

In the next chapter, we'll explore how brands evolve—how to adapt, grow, and reinvent your presence over time while keeping your identity intact. Because the best brands don't just stay consistent; they stay alive.

9

Chapter 9: The Evolution of a Brand—Staying Relevant in a Changing World

Growing up in small-town Indiana in the 1980s, you had your hangout spots. For me, eating out wasn't just an occasional treat—it was a way of life. My mom passed when I was fifteen, my older sister moved out shortly after, and Dad worked second shift. That meant a lot of dinners for one. And by "a lot," I mean **a lot**.

Salem didn't have many chain restaurants back then, so I developed my own lineup of local favorites—each with its own "Trueblood special." I'd pull into the drive-thru and hear, "Trueblood's here for his keel!" before I even said a word. (For the record, the "keel" was a chicken breast... and yes, it was amazing.)

Each of those spots had a distinct personality—what I now know was their brand. Most were incredibly friendly and equally familiar. These 'Go-To' spots were staples in my teenage world—places I thought would be around forever.

Wrong.

On a recent trip home, I realized that almost all of them were gone. The buildings had been replaced by fast-food chains or left vacant altogether. It wasn't the food or the service that did them in—it was time. They did everything "right" by 80s standards, but the calendar had flipped forward...the market had evolved...and they had not.

New restaurants came along with slick branding, QR-code menus, loyalty apps, and curbside pickup. They weren't necessarily cooking better food—but they made it easier for customers to order, pay, and connect. The world changed. The brands that survived changed with it. The ones that didn't? Well, they disappeared.

Change is tough, but standing still is tougher. My five go-to restaurants—two pizza joints, two chicken spots, and a burger place—all went dark because they failed to evolve.

Now, contrast that with a local cigar shop we've worked with for years. Same small-town roots, but a totally different mindset. They saw **change** coming and leaned into it. They didn't abandon who they were—far from it. They modernized who they were.

With a noticeable tweak, their logo was modernized. Further, they streamlined their messaging, and built an online ordering system (which wasn't easy, since cigars are an age-restricted product online). Their tagline, "Kick Back and Relax," reminded locals they were still the same reliable neighbor—just easier to reach.

The result? New faces, repeat customers, and a brand that felt fresh again without losing its soul.

That's the balance every business must strike: **Consistency builds trust. Evolution keeps that trust relevant.** Our world is not static. It is ever-changing. Your brand simply can't live in the "good old days," no matter how good they were. It has to live where your customers live—today, tomorrow, and wherever the future takes them.

The best brands never stand still. They honor where they've been but keep moving toward where their customers are going.

That's the thing about brands—they don't disappear overnight. They fade slowly, one unreturned customer at a time, one missed opportunity, one refusal to adapt. Just like those restaurants back home, a brand can quietly lose its relevance while still believing everything's fine. That's why evolution isn't optional; it's survival.

The good news? You don't have to reinvent your brand to evolve it. Actually, you probably should **not** do that. Reinvention is not evolution. You just have to recognize when the world—and your audience—have shifted, and make sure your story, visuals, and customer experience shift with them. That's what we'll dig into next: the laws of brand evolution—how to grow, modernize, and stay relevant without losing what made your brand special in the first place.

The Law of Brand Evolution

Brands are living things. They grow, they age, and if ignored long enough, they fade. Just like people, they need a little care, a few tune-ups, and the occasional wardrobe change to stay relevant. You can't freeze a brand in time and expect it to keep connecting. The market won't let you.

Think of evolution as not just a principle of branding, but a **law**—it's not optional. Everything changes: technology, trends, customer expectations, even how people communicate.

Remember MCI? Imagine telling their dinner-time telemarketer that you don't need long distance service. Communication has evolved, right? Thirty years ago, you were constantly toggling between AT&T, MCI and Sprint while haggling over those five cent per minute rates. Now? Nobody pays for long distance within the US today. The culture has evolved...technology with it and so to, brands.

Further on the communication side, we each hold a device that can do just about everything. Although more and more, the one thing we don't ask our smartphones to do is make phone calls! People text more than talk. Actually, among Millennials and Gen Z, 75 percent prefer to text rather than actually speak with someone.

And communication is just one aspect of the ebb and flow of our shifting culture. Technological advancements... social movements...economic and workplace changes—did anyone ever think working from home would be a popular option decades ago? And there are so many other changes in our society that impact a brand. Ignoring any of those shifts can be costly. What's more costly? Standing still.

When you don't evolve, you create a gap that competitors are all too happy to fill. After all, if they're the new kid on the block, you know they will want to look the part. They'll come in looking sharper, sounding fresher, and connecting in ways that make your once-loyal customers wonder if maybe you're the one who's changed. Spoiler alert: **you have**—you just didn't mean to.

If your brand doesn't evolve with them, it quietly becomes a relic. Not because it failed necessarily, but because it stood still while everything else moved forward.

And yet, resistance is common. I've lost count of how many times I've heard, "But we've always done it this way." Business owners often fear that change means losing what their customers loved in the first place. That's a fair concern. It is. People rail against change. But the reality is, your customers **have** changed too. Their needs, habits, and communication styles evolve constantly. What they once loved about your brand might now need a fresh coat of paint—or a complete remodel—just to keep them engaged.

So, how do you **evolve the right way?** The goal isn't reinvention—it's alignment. You stay true to your core purpose while modernizing the way you express it. Keep your roots, but refresh your branches. If your logo feels tired, maybe an easy tweak will keep continuity but brighten it up. If your messaging feels dated, simplify it. If your customer experience feels cumbersome, streamline it. Evolution doesn't mean abandoning your brand; it means making sure it still fits who your customers are today.

At BrandVision Marketing, we call this "smart evolution." It's about listening to the market, looking honestly at how your brand is perceived, and making intentional adjustments that **strengthen**—not replace—your identity. The best brands in the world—from Coca-Cola to your favorite local coffee shop—have mastered this balance. They don't chase trends. They adapt to them **with purpose**.

The bottom line? Brands that evolve stay relevant. Brands that resist change eventually become nostalgia—which may be great for your brand-themed memorabilia room, but nostalgia doesn't pay the bills. Consistency builds trust. Evolution within that continuity keeps that trust relevant.

🔊 *True Story*...I don't have to look far to find an example of a brand that's evolved — I just look in the mirror. BrandVision Marketing began as a traditional advertising agency, focused on TV, radio, outdoor, print, and direct mail campaigns. Had we stayed there, we'd be obsolete today. There's a reason those channels are now dubbed "traditional."

But we didn't stay there. We evolved.

First, we expanded into printing and promotional products to better serve client needs. Then, as digital began reshaping the marketing landscape, we dove in—offering SEO, website development, and social media strategy. Each step wasn't random; it was guided by our clients' evolving challenges and how we could solve them.

By constantly adapting, we've been able to remain what we've always wanted to be: an extension of our clients' marketing departments. We speak and wear their brand voice, lighten their load, and keep their message consistent across every channel—traditional or digital.

That's the point. Evolution doesn't mean changing who you are; it means staying relevant to the people you serve. Your brand's evolution should always be market-driven, strategically focused, and ultimately—customer-beneficial.

Signs It's Time for a Refresh

Brand evolution rarely happens overnight—it's usually a whisper before it's a shout. The signs are there if you're willing to listen. Lean in. Because the challenge most business owners face is being too close to their brand to spot the clues until the foghorn is blaring.

You might not need a total rebrand. In fact, you probably don't. You might just need to evolve—freshen your look, clarify your message, modernize your channels, or better align with your audience's expectations. But if you ignore those early signals, your brand can quietly slide into irrelevance while you're still patting yourself on the back for "staying consistent."

There are signs to watch for—little indicators that whisper, "It's time." Here are a few of the biggest:

1. Your customers have changed—but your brand hasn't.

Maybe you started out serving one audience, but that audience has aged, relocated, or shifted priorities. If your messaging still speaks to who they were ten years ago, you're missing who they are now—and who your new customers could be.

We worked with a small, highly niched credit union that wanted growth but refused to invest in real marketing. Every year, they'd say they wanted to expand, but relied solely on referrals and a shoestring budget. Membership numbers told the real story: +4...-2...+7...+2. That's not growth—that's a slow fade. When pressed, they'd shrug and say, "Well, some members pass away, so it balances out." But that's not balance—that's decline.

The problem wasn't their product or service—it was their perspective. Their audience had changed. The once-tight-knit community that fueled word-of-mouth now consumed media online, scrolled through social feeds, and made financial decisions after a quick Google search. Their brand hadn't evolved to meet that new behavior.

Decades ago, their referral circle might have sustained them. But today, digital marketing allows even a small niche to reach new members through hyper-targeted campaigns. The opportunity was sitting right there, waiting for them. But instead of adapting, they clung to the past.

For them, brand evolution didn't mean a new logo or slogan—it meant embracing a new way of connecting. Years ago, a $1,000 ad budget might have meant 97 percent wasted coverage for such a niche. Now, that same $1,000 could be used to reach precisely the right prospects—efficiently and repeatedly.

Evolving their brand wasn't about abandoning who they were; it was about showing up where their members actually are today.

2. Your competitors look sharper, faster, or more relevant.

If your competitors' brands feel more current—visually, verbally, or digitally—take note. This isn't about chasing trends; it's about staying competitive in perception.

And perception is reality.

A slight modernization—a refreshed logo, updated color palette, or simplified layout—can make a world of difference.

We updated our own BrandVision Marketing logo after 22 years. We didn't scrap it; we evolved it. Same typography. Same recognizable red triangle. We just added depth and dimension—a subtle 3D polish that modernized the look without losing the legacy. That's evolution—familiar but fresh.

3. You're apologizing for your website or materials.

If you've ever said, "We're working on updating that," you already know—it's past due. The moment you explain away your brand assets, your audience hears, "We're behind."

One local family law attorney understood this perfectly. We had done his website a few years prior. It was polished, but he told us, "I want to stay ahead of the curve—by next year, it might not be." That's smart branding. He wasn't reacting to being outdated—he was proactively evolving to stay relevant. No overhaul required. Just a slight freshening up that spoke with relevance to his core audience. We created a new site for him that has stayed true to his brand while sparking his desired pertinence.

4. You've expanded your services or shifted focus.

Growth is great—but if your offerings have evolved without your brand keeping pace, customers can't connect the dots.

A local utility company was known for gas, water, and electric. They expanded their services to add fiber-optic internet. Interesting, right? The problem? No one made the connection. In the customer's mind, they were a utility company, not a communications provider. That disconnect made growth more difficult and far more expensive than it had to be.

Your brand can evolve successfully—but only when new offerings fit neatly under the same umbrella of trust and understanding.

5. Your brand has stalled and staled in the market.

If your brand no longer inspires you, it probably doesn't inspire your audience either. When your materials feel stale, your energy follows—and your prospects and employees feel that. (Remember, your branding efforts always exist to keep your brand ambassadors engaged, too)

Now, I'm not suggesting you reinvent your look every few months because you're bored. By the time you're tired of your campaign, the market is just beginning to notice it. Continuity is a pillar of building a successful brand. But that brand should inspire you and your team. It should connect with the market. If it's stagnant—if you're not proud to show it off—that's a problem. Evolution reignites enthusiasm from the inside out.

The key takeaway? Don't wait for the market to force your hand. The best brands evolve with the market and by design, not desperation. They monitor shifts in culture, technology, and behavior—and adapt with strategy and purpose.

So, before your brand starts collecting dust, ask yourself:

- ➤ Does my message still resonate?
- ➤ Are we addressing Pain Points resolutely and effectively or has our message stalled?
- ➤ Do my visuals still represent who we are? Are they current?

> ➤ Are we still relevant to the customers we most want to reach?

If the answer isn't a confident "yes," it's time to start planning your evolution. Because if your marketing looks like a time capsule, your customers might think your products belong in one.

Refresh vs. Rebrand: How to Evolve Without Losing Your Identity

When business slows or competition heats up, the knee-jerk reaction is often, "We need a rebrand." But most of the time, you don't need to throw the baby out with the branding bathwater — you just need to add a few bubbles.

A refresh refines your existing identity; a rebrand replaces it. The difference between the two is often the difference between a revitalized business and a confused audience.

A refresh keeps what's working — building on your equity, your recognition, your hard-earned trust — and polishes the rest. Think of it like remodeling a house. You might repaint, swap out the fixtures, replace vinyl with hardwood, or even knock down a non-load-bearing wall, but you don't tear down the whole structure. The foundation stays the same; it just gets updated to fit modern living.

A rebrand, on the other hand? Bring in the bulldozer! It's a full rebuild. New logo, new colors, new message, new voice — often a revised focus and a new purpose. It's a big deal. We're not tweaking, we're re-constructing. And it's necessary only when your business has changed so dramatically that your old brand no longer is profitable or represents who you are. Mergers, major shifts in offerings, or a damaged reputation can call for a complete overhaul. But for most brands? A strategic refresh keeps you both familiar and relevant.

Here's a quick way to tell which one you might need:

You need a refresh if...

> ➢ Your visual identity feels dated, but still recognizable.
> ➢ Your message needs clarity, not reinvention.
> ➢ Your audience still knows and trusts you — you just need to re-energize them.
> ➢ Cash flow? It's still there, but you've noticed impacts in certain product/service lines that have you raising your eyebrows.

You might need a rebrand if...

> ➢ Your business model or target audience has changed entirely. In other words, your offering no longer fits neatly under the same brand umbrella.
> ➢ Your name or reputation no longer reflects your mission.
> ➢ Your brand equity is so diluted or confused that it's holding you back.
> ➢ Revenue streams? They're dwindling to the point of dysfunction.

At BrandVision Marketing, we've seen both ends of the spectrum. One local pub and hangout spot needed a complete rebrand. They had begun to attract a less than profitable crowd and a more than problematic pack. They needed to pull the plug and start over. Meanwhile, a Main Street credit union came to us convinced they needed a full rebrand as well. After a little digging, we realized the problem wasn't the brand — it was the presentation. Specifically, it suffered from a lack of focus and continuity from touchpoint to touchpoint. Their logo had strong local recognition, but their messaging was scattered, their visuals dated, and their tone inconsistent across platforms. That lack of continuity and blurred focus had created confusion among members and the locals. They didn't need to rebrand. A thoughtful refresh —unifying the message and tightening visuals — brought their brand roaring back to life. Within a year, they were the fastest growing credit union in the state. No rebrand needed.

Here's the thing: Evolution doesn't mean erasing your past. It means building on it with intention. Honor your history. After all, your brand's history is a source of credibility — proof that you've delivered for years and expect to for many more. Don't abandon that equity; amplify it. Accentuate it. It's a strong asset to be proud of.

Remember: people crave familiarity wrapped in freshness. "New" is always big in the market, right! A successful brand evolution feels like the same great friend, just wearing a new jacket. You still recognize them immediately, but you can't help noticing how sharp they look.

So before you swing the wrecking ball, pause. Assess. Ask yourself: Do we need a new identity, or just a new perspective?

Most of the time, the answer isn't "start over." No. Rather the solution is "start evolving." Not every brand needs a full body makeover. Sometimes, a fresh haircut and a new suit will more than do the trick.

How to Evolve Without Losing Your Core

One of the biggest fears business owners have when refreshing their brand is this: "If we change too much, will people still recognize us?"

Fair question. And the concern is understandable and real. After all, people in general do not like change. How often do you go to a favorite website to place yet another order, only to find that everything has changed…again! Well, except your eye-roll out of frustration for having to re-learn a new way to order, shop or connect? It's maddening. I get it. And you want to avoid those eye-roll moments with your customers while continuing to push forward.

But let's face it: nothing in this world is static. It is a world that moves, evolves, advances constantly. "Change is a constant." (And that little axiom is from the sage guy who brought us the Campbell Soup Cans!)

Your brand is something you've poured yourself into— time, sweat, and probably more than a few sleepless nights. But the reality is simple: evolution isn't about abandoning your brand; it's about making sure your brand keeps up with your audience while staying anchored to what made it special in the first place.

Back to the home metaphor--You don't tear down the whole house every few years. No—you remodel, repaint, and maybe new cabinets for the kitchen. The foundation? It stays the same. And your brand is that foundation. Your brand's evolution gives the locals an experience that feels new, relevant, and welcoming again.

Keep Your Brand Anchored in Its Purpose and Values

Before you change anything—logo, tagline, or tone—
revisit your brand's **why**. Why do you exist? What problem
do you solve better than anyone else? What Pain Points are
you addressing? What emotions do you want people to feel
when they interact with you? Those answers form your
anchor. Without them, change becomes misdirected chaos.
With them, it becomes a finely tuned machine.

Audit Your Brand Regularly

At least once a year, take an honest look at your brand from
every angle: visuals, messaging, voice and tone, and
customer experience. Ask:

> ➤ Do all touchpoints still align?
> ➤ Does our look still feel modern and relevant?
> ➤ Is our message still resonating with the people we
> most want to reach?

Sometimes you'll just need a fresh coat of paint. Other
times, you'll realize the neighborhood has changed—and
you need to update the house a bit more.

Engage Your Team and Customers

Your employees and customers are your best barometers of
change. They experience your brand every day. Ask them

what they think still feels strong—and what feels stale.
What works? What no longer fits the bill?

You don't have to crowdsource your direction, but listening
helps ensure you evolve with your audience, not away from
them. Keep in mind, I'm not suggesting you talk to one
employee or one customer and treat those opinions like a
sample size of a thousand. No. But you can engage with
numerous people who live the brand or interact with it
routinely and use that as a smart gauge moving forward.

Roll Out Updates with a Clear Narrative

When you do evolve, don't just unveil the new look—tell
the story behind it. Frame it as progress, not departure.

- ➢ "Here's how we've grown."
- ➢ "Here's what we've learned."
- ➢ "Here's why these changes matter to you and how
  they will help you moving forward."

People respond to honesty and purpose; especially if it's
beneficial for them long-term. When they understand why
you evolved, they're more likely to embrace the change
instead of questioning it…and worse, railing against it.

🔊 *True Story*…A local community bank we worked with
had been around for nearly 20 years. Their name was
familiar, their logo recognizable, and their reputation
steady. But something wasn't clicking. The advertising had
grown stale—using generic slogans about "great customer
service" that could've come from any financial institution
in town. The result? Ads that neither attracted new

customers nor delivered that much-desired feel good message for their current patrons. It all pointed to wasted marketing dollars, which is **never** good.

When we sat down with the president, the apprehensions were understandable. "We don't want our longtime customers to think we're totally different," he told me. Fair concern—but staying exactly the same wasn't preserving their brand, it was aging it.

As we dug deeper, we uncovered another issue: a well-intentioned public relations program that highlighted one student each month from a specific school. It came with consistent photo ops and news coverage. So, great idea, right? Yes. Except the bank served twelve schools across the county. What started as a goodwill initiative had quietly turned into a PR blind spot. It made that one school feel special and eleven others feel ignored. Welcome to Main Street, right! Simply put: it meant delivering one 'warm and fuzzy' to eleven, "Hmm…why not us?" Not a good ratio.

We didn't tear anything down—we just widened the lens. The PR program was expanded to include all the county schools, turning an exclusionary perception into a unifying one and a true PR victory. Then, we refined the messaging, building a campaign around what truly set them apart: reliability, trust, and genuine community connection. The new tagline struck that balance perfectly—it felt familiar, but freshly relevant.

The results came fast. The bank's ads regained meaning and confidence. Their digital platforms finally looked and sounded cohesive. Even employees got on board with renewed pride. And those longtime customers? They didn't feel alienated—they felt proud. One told the president, "I like it! You're still you—just look newer." (He took that to mean 'younger', which was a big plus to that particular 74-year-old CEO!)

That's exactly the goal: Positive community goodwill! The strongest brands don't abandon their roots—they nurture them, prune what's overgrown, and keep evolving in ways that make their audience fall in love with them all over again.

Your brand's foundation—your purpose, promise, and personality—should never waver. But the way you express it will always need to be met with growth, adaptation, and relevance. Change too little or not at all, and you fade. Change too much, and you lose yourself. The magic is in the middle—evolving just enough to remind your audience why they loved you in the first place

Future-Proofing Your Brand

The brands that last aren't the biggest or the loudest—they're the most adaptable.

Think about it. A decade ago, few would've guessed that influencer marketing, short-form video, or AI-driven personalization would so greatly impact the marketing culture. Yet here we are. And ten years from now, we'll probably be saying the same thing about something we haven't even heard of yet.

Now, before you freak out at that thought, as admittedly I did a smidge…realize this: Treating the evolution of your brand as a **constant**, meets that always changing aspect of the business culture. That's why the key to future-proofing your brand isn't predicting every new trend—it's building adaptability **into** your brand.

Too many businesses treat branding as a "set it and forget it" exercise. They develop a logo, lock in some messaging, and then treat any change as a threat to stability. Now, if you've read this far you know how vital I believe continuity is to a successful brand, right? It's one of the three staples (Distinction/Relevance/Continuity). But evolution isn't the enemy of consistency—it's the engine that keeps consistency relevant. You want a brand that can grow, shift, and respond to culture without losing its core DNA.

The most successful brands stay humble and curious. They listen—to customers, to data, to shifts in behavior and technology. They don't panic when a new platform emerges or an old one fades away. They explore, experiment, and learn. They know their core purpose but remain flexible in how they express it.

That's what adaptability looks like.

When streaming TV emerged, local businesses could have easily dismissed it as "for the big guys." Instead, the smart ones leaned in, learning to use connected TV and OTT ads to target audiences with surgical precision—getting national-level exposure without the national-level budget. Not to mention the wasted dollars of network TV or radio spent to promote to audiences you have no interest in reaching. The technology changed, but the goal didn't: get in front of the right people with the right message at the right time.

Future-proofing your brand doesn't mean chasing every shiny object that comes along. It means having the awareness to recognize what truly adds value to your customers and what just adds noise.

So, ask yourself:

> ➤ Is our team open to new ideas and learning from change?
> ➤ Do we regularly evaluate how technology impacts our customer experience?
> ➤ Are we clear enough on our purpose to evolve our methods without losing who we are?

The future of your brand doesn't rely on having all the answers—it's about staying curious enough to keep asking the right questions.

Because at the end of the day, the brands that endure don't just adapt to the world—they help shape what comes next.

Conclusion: The Brand That Keeps Becoming

Change? It's not your enemy—it's just our culture's environment. It's omnipresent so the brands that thrive aren't the ones that cling to the past or chase every new trend. No. They're the brands that evolve with purpose. They honor their heritage while adapting to meet the present moment. They keep their core intact while updating how that core is expressed and how it maintains its relevance with the audience.

When your brand evolves intentionally and with purpose, it does more than survive—it strengthens. It reminds your customers that you're not stuck in time; you're moving right alongside them. The brands that win tomorrow are those that stay curious, stay listening, and stay aligned with what their audience truly values.

After all, your brand is a living, breathing story—one that evolves as you do. The moment you stop learning from your customers, your community, and your craft… your brand stops growing. But when you commit to staying authentic, curious, and connected, your brand never grows old—it just keeps becoming.

Because at the end of the day, evolution isn't about reinvention—it's about *relevance.*

In the next chapter, we'll bring everything full circle. We'll step back from the day-to-day and look at the **complete BrandVision Marketing Local Branding Blueprint**—a process that connects clarity, consistency, culture, and communication into one cohesive system. You'll see how every piece you've worked through so far—your research, your message, your voice, your training, your digital presence, your adaptability—fits together to create something profitably enduring.

Because branding isn't just about being known today. It's about building something worth remembering tomorrow.

10

Chapter 10: The Blueprint for Brand Longevity

If you've made it this far—kudos, my friend. You've explored what makes a brand stand out and what keeps it standing strong.

Now you know: great brands aren't accidents. They're built intentionally—layer by layer, decision by decision, touchpoint by touchpoint.

Building a brand is well, like writing a book. You take a concept that addresses someone's need. You research…like crazy. You put together the nuts and bolts…write and rewrite, and add the character that makes it uniquely you. But brands are not meant to sit on desks—they are living structures that evolve over time.

The process begins with identifying a profitable direction— we call that **BrandFOCUS**. That means understanding the Pain Points your customers face and positioning your brand as the solution.

Next is **BrandTRAINING**—educating the people who bring your brand to life every day. Employees become your brand's ambassadors, shaping every interaction with authenticity and purpose.

Finally, through **BrandPLAN**, you craft a communications strategy that connects your message to the right audience—

using the right mix of traditional and digital media to deliver impact.

Together, these stages define who your brand is at its core and move that truth front and center, creating a relationship that feels genuine and consistent. Because trying to be something you're not? That's the fastest way to send consumers sprinting to a competitor.

BrandVision Marketing's Local Branding Blueprint Recap

The BrandVision Marketing Local Branding Blueprint isn't theory—it's a living, breathing framework that adapts to any business, any market, any era. Whether you're building from scratch, revitalizing a legacy, or scaling what's already working, the blueprint holds steady.

Every principle and story in this book connects to one of the 8 C's—core components that drive brand success:

- ➤ **Clarity** – Know who you are, what you do, and why it matters. Confused customers don't buy; confused employees don't sell.
- ➤ **Consistency** – Show up the same way everywhere. Familiarity breeds trust; inconsistency breeds doubt.
- ➤ **Culture** – Your people are your brand. When they live it, customers feel it.
- ➤ **Connection** – Speak to emotion first, logic second. Relationships build brands—which translate into much more than transactions.
- ➤ **Communication** – Align every message and medium with your mission.
- ➤ **Credibility** – Deliver what you promise, and promise what you can deliver. Authenticity wins

every time. Overpromising is a great way to lose this 'C'.

➢ **Continuity** – Bridge your message seamlessly from physical to digital touchpoints.

➢ **Change** – Evolve with intention. The strongest brands adapt without losing their essence.

Eight simple ideas. Eight powerful levers. Taken together, they build a brand that's both profitable and unshakably authentic.

A Living Brand Never Stands Still

The market will shift. Technology will evolve. Your audience will grow and change.

That's not something to fear—it's something to prepare for.

A future-ready brand doesn't chase every shiny new object; it adapts with purpose. It stays curious, self-aware, and grounded in what makes it real.

Your blueprint isn't a static plan—it's a living document. Revisit it and refine it as needed.

Just as a builder checks the plans before every new phase, revisit your brand regularly and ask:

➢ Does our message still align with our mission?
➢ Do our people still reflect our purpose?
➢ Are we still connecting where our customers spend their time?

If not—adjust. That's how you stay relevant without losing who you are.

The Final Word

My goal for this book is simple. I want to reach owners of small to mid-size local businesses—those who are maybe up against tough competition with deeper pockets. Because you know what? That's where I've been time and time again. Working with the little guy—the community bank with five locations going up against state institutions with hundreds; the 2-attorney law firm facing conglomerate firms seeking to simply outspend competitors into submission; independent insurance agents who are up against well-known brands with instant name recognition and hefty budgets.

So, my goal for this book? I want it to be read, of course. But I want it to sit on those business owner's desks as a reference guide anytime they come across a pertinent question that impacts their brand. Because they know, if they've followed this blueprint, they can count on this book for good advice.

A strong brand doesn't just exist in the marketplace—it impacts it, providing a distinguishable, resilient voice. Because…and total transparency here…I have worked with hundreds of brands, but no market leaders. But you don't have to be number one in a category to be relevant. Good brands know that **profitability** is always the goal. And creating your brand with distinction, relevance and continuity versus the competition will make that happen. Plain and simple.

You see, a brand doesn't just tell a story—it lives one. It lives a tale that connects and furthers a relationship that resonates for years to come.

And it doesn't just sell products—it builds belief.

Because branding isn't just about logos, taglines, or ad campaigns.

Sure all of those matter. Yes. But it's more. It's about trust, relationship, and reputation—all built over time, one interaction at a time…with each and every touchpoint.

If you can remember just one thing from this book, let it be this:

Your brand isn't what you say it is. Remember our manila folder analogy? Keep it front and center—because with every interaction, your customers are building a narrative for your brand that lives in that manila folder of their mind. So, ultimately? Your brand is what people remember it to be.

Keep helping them add to that memory…thickening that manila folder—one clear message, one authentic interaction, and one bold decision at a time.

How do you build a brand that will last? You build a relationship that will last.

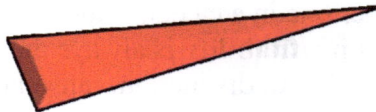

THE BRANDVISION BLUEPRINT

BrandFOCUS

Discovering direction... finding your brand's voice and detailing your messaging to address Pain Pointsand communicate your USP

BrandTRAINING

Living the brand

BrandPLAN

Develop your communications plan to target your consumers... utilizing various methods from Traditional to Digital to connect with your prospects

Evolution

Staying relevant

Appendix A

Brand Message Clarity Checklist

5 Core Elements of Clear Messaging

- 1. The Problem You Solve – Speak directly to pain points.

- 2. Your Solution – Show how you remove the pain.

- 3. Value/Outcome – Paint the after-picture.

- 4. Why You? – Clarify your distinction.

- 5. Clear Call-to-Action – Tell them what to do next.

6 Pitfalls to Avoid

- Feature-Laden Messaging – specs without emotion.

- Jargon Overload – confusing instead of clarifying.

- Too Many Messages – nothing sticks.

- Copycat Syndrome – blending in, not standing out.

- Inconsistent Messaging – ad vs. experience mismatch.

- Weak or Missing CTA – no clear next step.

Quick Test

➡ Can a stranger understand what problem you solve, how you solve it, and what to do next in under 5 seconds? If not, refine until the answer is YES.

BRANDVISION
MARKETING

📕 Sources & Citations

Chapter 1: What is a Brand Really?

- Aaker, David. *Building Strong Brands.* Free Press, 1996.
- Keller, Kevin Lane. *Strategic Brand Management: Building, Measuring, and Managing Brand Equity.* Pearson, 2013.
- Neumeier, Marty. *The Brand Gap: How to Bridge the Distance Between Business Strategy and Design.* New Riders, 2006.
- Interbrand. "Best Global Brands 2023 Report." Interbrand Group, 2023.

Chapter 2: Brand Strategy: Define Before You Design

- Kotler, Philip, and Kevin Lane Keller. *Marketing Management.* Pearson, 2016.
- Harvard Business Review. "What Great Brands Do Differently." HBR, 2021.
- Nielsen, Norman Group. "User Research Basics." 2022.
- Sprout Social. "Social Media Demographics and Usage Statistics." 2023.

Chapter 3: Building a Brand Identity that Connects

- Wheeler, Alina. *Designing Brand Identity: An Essential Guide for the Whole Branding Team.* Wiley, 2020.
- Neumeier, Marty. *Zag: The Number One Strategy of High-Performance Brands.* New Riders, 2007.
- Adobe Creative Cloud Blog. "Visual Consistency in Branding." 2022.

Chapter 4: Clarifying Your Brand Message

- Miller, Donald. *Building a StoryBrand: Clarify Your Message So Customers Will Listen.* HarperCollins Leadership, 2017.
- Godin, Seth. *This Is Marketing: You Can't Be Seen Until You Learn to See.* Portfolio, 2018.
- Psychology Today. "Why Emotional Marketing Works." 2021.
- BrandVision Marketing Internal Framework: BrandFOCUS™ Model (Unpublished Proprietary Material).

Chapter 5: Avoiding Common Messaging Blunders

- Cialdini, Robert. *Influence: The Psychology of Persuasion.* Harper Business, 2006.
- Nielsen Norman Group. "The Power of Microcopy: How Small Words Make a Big Impact." 2020.
- BrandVision Marketing Case Studies (2020–2024).

Chapter 6: The Psychology of Branding

- Sinek, Simon. *Start with Why: How Great Leaders Inspire Everyone to Take Action.* Portfolio, 2009.
- Harvard Business Review. "Culture Is the Brand." HBR, 2019.
- BrandVision Marketing Training Framework: BrandTRAINING™ (Internal Document).

Chapter 7: Continuity: Branding Across Touchpoints

- Google Ads. "Smart Bidding and Ad Quality Overview." 2023.

- WordStream. "The Ultimate Guide to PPC for Small Business." 2022.
- HubSpot Research. "Ad Fatigue and Consumer Trust." 2023.
- BrandVision Marketing Paid Search Case Files (2019–2024).

Chapter 8: Branding in the Digital Era

- Edelman Trust Barometer. "The State of Trust in Digital Media." 2023.
- Pew Research Center. "How Americans Use Social Media in 2023."
- BrandVision Marketing Case Study: Personal Injury Law Firm (2022).
- *[1] https://capitaloneshopping.com/research/online-vs-in-store-shopping-statistics/; May 2025.
- Moz. "Local SEO Ranking Factors." 2023.

Chapter 9: The Evolution of a Brand—Staying Relevant in a Changing World

- Ries, Al, and Jack Trout. *Positioning: The Battle for Your Mind.* McGraw-Hill, 2001.
- Harvard Business Review. "Why Great Brands Evolve—And How They Stay True." 2020.
- StudyFinds.org: https://studyfinds.org/millennials-gen-z-communicate-texting/
- BrandVision Marketing Case Study: Community Bank Campaign (2021).
- BrandVision Marketing Case Study: Local Credit Union Analysis (2020–2023).

Chapter 10: The Blueprint for Longevity

- BrandVision Marketing Proprietary Model: BrandFOCUS™, BrandTRAINING™, BrandPLAN™.
- Collins, Jim. *Good to Great: Why Some Companies Make the Leap and Others Don't.* Harper Business, 2001.
- McKinsey & Company. "Building Brands That Last in the Digital Age." 2022.

Additional Recommended Reading

- Neumeier, Marty. *The Brand Flip.* New Riders, 2015.
- Keller, Kevin Lane. *Best Practice Cases in Branding.* Pearson, 2019.
- Godin, Seth. *Purple Cow: Transform Your Business by Being Remarkable.* Portfolio, 2003.
- Scott, David Meerman. *The New Rules of Marketing and PR.* Wiley, 2020.
- Holt, Douglas. *Cultural Strategy: Using Innovative Ideologies to Build Breakthrough Brands.* Oxford University Press, 2010.

I recommend any and all of the books found throughout the citations. They sit keenly in my office bookshelf and several have been read...and re-read... a few times!

📕 List of Definitions

A

A/B Testing – Comparing two versions of an ad, webpage, or campaign to see which performs better based on real data (for example, testing two headlines to see which drives more clicks).

Ad Impressions – The number of times an ad is displayed to a user, regardless of whether it's clicked.

Algorithm – The automated process used by digital platforms (like Google or Facebook) to determine what content users see.

Authenticity – The degree to which a brand is perceived as real, honest, and consistent with its values and promises.

B

Brand – The total perception people have of your business—built from every experience, message, and touchpoint.

Brand Ambassadors – Employees or advocates who represent and reinforce your brand's values and personality in every interaction.

Brand Consistency – Maintaining uniformity in messaging, visuals, and tone across every platform or customer touchpoint.

Brand Equity – The value your brand holds in the minds of consumers, shaped by recognition, reputation, and trust.

Brand Evolution – The process of refining and modernizing your brand over time without losing its core identity.

Brand Identity – The collection of visual and verbal elements—logo, color palette, typography, imagery, tagline, and tone—that express who you are.

Brand Loyalty – When customers consistently choose your brand over competitors, often driven by emotional connection rather than price.

Brand Voice – The distinct personality and tone your brand uses to communicate, whether in social posts, ads, or customer service.

BrandFOCUS – BrandVision Marketing's discovery process for identifying your most profitable market direction and brand purpose.

BrandPLAN – The structured communication strategy that aligns your messaging, media, and marketing efforts toward measurable goals.

BrandTRAINING – The process of teaching your employees how to "live the brand" by embodying its message and values in every customer interaction.

C

Call to Action (CTA) – A phrase that encourages the audience to take a specific next step (e.g., "Sign up today," "Call now," or "Learn more").

Click-Through Rate (CTR) – The percentage of people who click on an ad or link after seeing it.

Color Palette – A defined set of colors that represent your brand visually and consistently across materials.

Continuity – The seamless connection between all touchpoints—online and offline—that ensures your brand feels cohesive everywhere it appears.

Conversion – When a user completes a desired action (such as making a purchase, filling out a form, or subscribing to an email list).

Customer Journey – The complete path a customer takes from awareness to consideration to purchase—and ideally, to loyalty.

D

Design System – A comprehensive guide that defines your brand's visual standards (colors, typography, imagery, spacing, etc.) to maintain consistency across all platforms.

Digital Footprint – The sum of your brand's presence and activity across digital platforms, including websites, social media, and reviews.

Differentiator (USP) – The unique aspect of your brand that sets you apart from competitors; your "reason to choose us."

E

Emotional Branding – The strategy of connecting with audiences through feelings, values, and emotional drivers rather than just features and price.

Engagement – How your audience interacts with your brand online (likes, comments, shares, clicks, etc.).

Evergreen Content – Marketing content that remains relevant and effective long after it's published.

F

Funnel (Marketing Funnel) – The model that maps the stages of a customer's journey—from Awareness → Consideration → Decision → Action → Loyalty.

G

Google My Business (GMB) – A free tool that allows local businesses to manage their online presence across Google Search and Maps.

I

Imagery Style – The specific look and feel of your brand's photos, illustrations, or videos that reflect its tone and personality.

Impression Share – The percentage of total available ad impressions your campaign captures compared to competitors.

K

Key Performance Indicators (KPIs) – Measurable metrics that track the success of your marketing efforts (such as leads generated, sales conversions, or website visits).

L

Landing Page – A standalone web page designed to drive a single action, like signing up for an offer or downloading a resource.

Logo – A brand's most recognizable visual identifier, often consisting of a symbol, typography, or combination of both.

M

Manila Folder of the Mind – Scott Trueblood's metaphor which describes how customers mentally organize and relate to their experiences and impressions of your brand over time.

Message Clarity – The ability for your audience to instantly understand who you are, what you do, and why it matters.

Micro-Moments – Small, intent-driven moments when consumers turn to their devices to learn, discover, or decide something quickly.

P

Pain Point – A specific problem or frustration your customer is experiencing and trying to solve.

Persona (Buyer Persona) – A semi-fictional profile representing your ideal customer based on research and data.

Positioning – The distinct space your brand occupies in the mind of your target audience compared to competitors.

Psychology of Branding – The study of how human emotions, perceptions, and subconscious triggers influence consumer behavior.

R

Rebranding – A complete overhaul of your brand's identity, often including name, logo, messaging, and positioning changes.

Referral Marketing – Encouraging existing customers to recommend your brand to others, often through incentives or rewards.

Reputation Management – Monitoring and influencing your brand's public perception—especially through reviews and online feedback.

S

SEO (Search Engine Optimization) – The process of optimizing your website to improve visibility and ranking in search engine results.

Social Proof – The psychological concept that people tend to follow the actions or opinions of others—such as reviews, testimonials, or endorsements.

StoryBrand Framework – A storytelling method developed by Donald Miller that positions the customer as the hero and the brand as the guide.

Style Guide – A written document outlining your brand's design rules, tone, and visual identity standards.

T

Tagline – A concise phrase that captures your brand's core promise or personality.

Target Audience – The specific group of people most likely to benefit from—and buy—your product or service.

Touchpoint – Any point of contact between your brand and the customer, online or offline.

Typography – The specific fonts and text styles used to express your brand's personality and maintain visual consistency.

U

USP (Unique Selling Proposition) – A clear statement that defines what makes your brand different and better in the marketplace.

UX (User Experience) – How a user interacts with your website or app, including ease of navigation, design flow, and satisfaction.

V

Value Proposition – The core statement explaining the benefit your brand delivers and why it's worth choosing.

Visual Identity – The combination of logo, color, typography, and imagery that makes your brand instantly recognizable.

W

Word-of-Mouth Marketing – Organic sharing of brand experiences between consumers—still one of the most powerful forms of promotion, now amplified through digital reviews and social media

---